BEYOND
ASSERTIVENESS

BEYOND ASSERTIVENESS

JOHN FAUL / DAVID AUGSBURGER

Calibre

Calibre Books/a division of Word Books, Publisher
Waco, Texas

BEYOND ASSERTIVENESS by John C. Faul and David Augsburger.
Copyright © 1980 by Word, Incorporated, Waco, TX 76796.
All rights reserved. No portion of this book may be reproduced in any
form whatsoever without written permission from the publisher.

ISBN 0–8499–2925–3
Library of Congress catalog card number: 80–51450
Printed in the United States of America

567898 MV 9876543

Contents

Preface

Asserting and affirming.

Leveling with another and loving the other.

Confronting with my needs and caring about yours.

Each of these pairs denotes the two sides of wholeness, of maturity, of growing personhood. Effective living occurs as skills in both self-assertion and self-affirmation are expressed with equal concern for the other person's rights and respect.

Assertiveness training that does not include affirmation teaching creates one-sided growth.

We need both. Thus this book is needed to integrate assertiveness with human relations skills, power, and love.

"Why one more book among the hundreds already written on becoming your own person?" Because it has something crucial and unique to offer—a creative integration of living skills with loving skills.

This book is neither a scientific treatise nor a book of popular reading for casual stimulation. It is written as a guide to new experiments in living and fresh experiences of being. The primary focus is on new behaviors in difficult situations through behavioral change. Attempt has been made to be scientifically accurate, but some liberty has been taken with the science. Meticulous scientific explanation has frequently been compromised to make the material more understandable and practical. We seek to keep the spirit rather than the law of science. We have tried to balance research data with pragmatism. Good science can be presented in a cold, factual, impersonal fashion which turns people off and loses more than it gains. Our goal has been to use scientific principles with as much humanness as we could achieve.

This book is an outgrowth of our work with the many people who have consulted us in time of need. As they have shared their pains and sorrows, they have taught us as much as we have taught them. They have taught us to share ourselves with them. It is in sharing ourselves with others that mutual growth occurs. Their encouragement to put into writing the understanding and insights of human behavior and human relationships that were mutually shared in the consulting room provided the first stimulus for this book.

In addition to clients, patients, associates, teachers, parents, and families who have contributed so much directly to the making of this book, there are many others who have contributed indirectly.

The writings of many people have shaped our thinking about behavioral change. Among these are Albert Bandura, Joseph Wolpe, Arnold Lazarus, L. P. Ulman, L. Krasner, Robert E. Alberti, Michael L. Emmons, D. Meichenbaum, Fritz Perls, Albert Ellis, Victor Frankl, and Paul Tournier. There are many other people who shaped much of our thinking to whom we owe a debt of gratitude.

We are most grateful to our wives, Eloise and Nancy, who have assisted with the manuscripts and to our daughters Annette and Ellynne, Deborah and Judith, who accepted authors' isolations from the family to write, and also offered their encouragement to see the project to completion.

And most of all, we are grateful to you who are joining us in the process of growth we are sharing in the chapters, exercises, and experiences of this book—conversation on loving and living powerfully with each other.

Introduction

How to use this book (or abuse this book)

This book is three books.
They can be read in any order.
They can be skipped, skimmed, or scrambled by reading sections of each.

BOOK ONE—WHAT—sets forth the benefits of assertive and affirmative living. It is a manifesto of freedom and fidelity—freedom to claim your rights as a person, fidelity to cherish your loving relationships with others. Read it to enrich your dream and expand your awareness of effective living.

BOOK TWO—HOW—is a primer on behavior change. Everything you need to know to understand how behavior is learned and relearned; how behavior functions and dysfunctions, how change is reinforced and rewarded.

BOOK THREE—HERE AND NOW—brings *what* and *how* together in a sequence of insights and exercises for your personal use and practice. It is an experiential guide for reinventing your responses to life here. Now.

Use the book any way you wish. It's been useful for both of us in celebrating new freedom and power in loving-living.

John Faul, M.D.
David Augsburger, Ph. D.

Book One.
WHAT?

What are affirmation, assertion, and wholeness?

Chapter 1.
ASSERT AND AFFIRM
Loving and Leveling
in Life-Relationships

Following the line of traffic into the restaurant parking lot, I find my way suddenly blocked by another car seeking to exit from what was being used as an entrance by a stream of cars.

"You're coming in the wrong way," the man yells, pointing at a small sign, blackened by road dirt. Sure enough. I am in the wrong. He is right. Angrily right. He climbs out of the car. The street lights shine on his clean-shaven head.

"What are you going to do about this?" he asks, aggressively.

"I'd like for you to back up six feet and let me through. I can hardly back out into the solid traffic on the street."

"You want me to do that?" he asks, taken off guard by my firm assertiveness. He's angry, and he's wanting to offer me all of his accumulated anger triggered by the whole stream of cars that have been blocking the entrance. I remain warm, and firm in requesting he let me pass. He returns to his car; I back to the side, then slowly pull past him as he exits. He is still obviously enraged. I have not made it easy for him to ventilate his anger on me.

I could have asked for his anger by being aggressive in return. Had I too climbed from my car and advanced with fists equally clenched, words similarly spiced, I would have been asking for him to unload his rage.

I might have acted weakly, placatingly, and invited his dumping his irritation on me by being easily intimidated. Rather, I gave no apology, made no defense. I pointed to the obvious danger of backing into the traffic; I asked for room to pass.

Aggressive behavior usually is self-defeating. It seldom achieves its own goals. By overreacting and overextending itself, the aggressive style sets itself up to fail. Threat produces counterthreat. Violence elicits violence.

Passive behavior is equally self-sabotaging. By playing weak, it sacrifices its own goals. By yielding before the fact it volunteers defeat. An unnecessary acquiescence undersells one's own strength and power.

Learning the art of assertiveness is a crucial step toward expressing your goals for relationship, and it is only half the process. Skills in loving and relationship building are equally crucial.

Affirmative skills—positive, powerful affectional skills— are necessary if any lasting relationships are to be created, nurtured, and celebrated with others.

Real loving skills and rich love supplies are needed to temper the sharp edge of assertiveness. The rise of assertiveness training books, seminars, and workshops in the recent past drew anxious, hesitant, avoidant people into quick learning of assertive techniques. Many became no more effective as human beings or authentically assertive as persons through the course of the training. In fact, the question can be raised whether it taught them much more than clever skills in being more defensive, more individualistic, more narcissistic, and more motivated by unenlightened self-interest. Substantial and long-lasting changes must be built on more than new assertive behavior patterns; they must be grounded in new loving behaviors and loving attitudes toward self and others. Such training promotes self-understanding and self-appreciation balanced by equal interest in understanding and appreciating others. Modifying nonassertive habits of behaving and thinking is a change to be made at an intrapersonal as well as interpersonal level. Authentic love of self and others must be developed at the same time as the exercise of power in relationships with oneself and with another. Love and power must be exercised together for justice to be done.

Assert!

If I will not assert my strength with others, I will exist on others' decency, gentleness, or support. I am at their disposal—or their indifference. I will be asking others to take the initiative for my living. I will be allowing them to live my life for me.

If I assert my strength in relationships with others, I can become *I*. I can act with power and dignity. Knowing I deserve respect, I can claim the respect of others. Realizing I can initiate the quality of relationships I want, I will act in a firm and gentle way with others and with myself. I can do it here, now, whether or not such a relationship of mutual respect and trust is understood between us in this moment. A new creative relationship of dignity begins with one person choosing it, claiming it, living it toward the other. I can assert myself and begin now. Here. With you.

Affirm!

If I will not affirm my worth, I will exist only on others' pity, kindness, or compassion. I am at their mercy—or their apathy. I will be asking them to take the initiative for my loving. I will be asking them to give love and value to my life. It can be a lonely wait.

If I affirm my worth and your equal worth as a person, I become *I*. I see you as *you*. Knowing I am worthful and unquestionably valuable, I will prize my worthfulness whether you recognize me at the moment or refuse to see me as the person of significance I know me to be. Realizing that you are of equal worth, I can value you as I value myself whether you are honoring your own dignity or not.

I can begin to prize you and me equally, whether or not you respect such equality and mutual reverence for persons at this moment. A loving relationship begins with one who loves, respects, prizes equally both self and others. I can affirm me. I can affirm you. I can love now. Here. With you.

Assert—Affirm!

Bill walks into my office stiffly. His face is a mask of anger frozen into helpless rage.

"Twenty minutes ago I answered my phone. It was my brother. And he just blew my whole Christmas vacation."

"'Hello, Bill,' he says. 'Surprise, Bill. We're all coming for Christmas. Be there tomorrow. In time for dinner. See you then.'"

"And what did you say?" I ask. He shrugs empty-handed. "Certainly you said something. It was a conversation, wasn't it?"

"Oh, I said, "Hi, huh? Uhhuh. Uh. Bye.' That's all. But I wanted to say, 'Hello, Jim. Whoa, Jim. No, Jim. Goodbye, Jim.' But I didn't."

"What stopped you?"

"Well, he's my brother. My little brother. I've always looked after him. I can't say no to him."

"Well, Merry Christmas!"

"Merry Christmas? We had the whole time planned. We want to be alone as a family for our celebration this year. We certainly don't want to be working and cooking and entertaining the whole weekend when these three days are the only vacation we have."

"What do you want to do, Bill? Run a hotel for your brother's family?"

"I want to say no. But I can't. He'd be terribly hurt."

I look at Bill's flat expression. I see the powerlessness in his eyes. He sees no options. He is beaten by the first 'Hello.'

If Bill were free to assert himself he might respond to his brother with a bit more honesty and candor: "Our Christmas is planned, Jim. We want to be alone this year. Our time is reserved for us as a family. So I'd suggest you go on to your contingency plans. Certainly you have several other options up your sleeve."

Asserting himself could free Bill from having his brother's

family intrude on his Christmas. But if it breaks down communication and breaks up family trust, it won't be a very happy Christmas for either family. Jim and family will be resentful. Bill and family may feel guilty. If so, both lose. For effective living, assertion is not enough. Assertion exercises the power to say no and yes to situations. Affirmation expresses the ability to say yes or no to relationships. When both are expressed in balanced integrity, both persons can win.

"Our Christmas is planned, Jim. We care about you folks and want to be with you, and we also want the three-day weekend for ourselves to do the things we've promised each other. Let's plan another time to get together—New Year's, Easter, or next summer. Can we plan something farther ahead, Jim?"

Affirmation of others builds relationship; assertiveness defines what the relationship can be. A balance of both builds trust, respect, and satisfaction for each party. Both can win.

Assert AND Affirm

When a person takes a positive or direct action toward tension or conflict, the tendency is to act either all assertively *or* all affirmatively—either one or the other. Each is ineffective by itself. Each is indispensable to the effective exercise of the other. Both must occur simultaneously for getting us what we want and where we want to be with others.

Assertiveness can get what we want—what we value and care about in our interchanges with others.

Affirmation can get us where we want to be—in open trusting relationships with others.

The signs of being nonassertive and nonaffirmative are similar, since they are two sides of the same behavioral reality. One is the negation of equal rights in the relationship; the other is the negation of equal respect for the relationship. Power and love negated into powerlessness and mistrust, helplessness and hopelessness. Read each column, and then compare.

Nonassertive Characteristics	*Nonaffirmative Characteristics*
He feels the rights of others are far more important than his own.	She feels others may deserve respect, but since she gets none, she gives none.
He hesitates to express any conflicting wishes, however legitimate.	She wishes others understood her, but fears to be open lest they hurt her.
He automatically placates others when he fears offending them.	She bad-mouths herself when embarrassed, labeling herself stupid, clumsy, dumb, no good.
He allows others to maneuver and manipulate his decisions.	She can't say no to any request, so she can offer only a guarded yes.
He feels constantly on trial when confronted by authority figures.	She puts herself down compulsively, or she brags and plays one-up defensively.
He is easily hurt by what others say and never forgets an insult or a slight.	She broods a lot about how insensitive others are and looks for evidence in their eyes.
He is often resentful inside, feeling pushed, used, taken advantage of.	She feels constantly guilty about anger, and angry that she is always guilty.
He gets depressed at unexpected times and can't put his finger on what's wrong.	She wants love and approval desperately. She refuses to give it until she gets it.
He feels constantly inferior; talks in self-depreciating terms.	She feels that she is truly worthless. "If they really knew me they wouldn't love me."

The excuses for staying nonassertive are, not surprisingly, similar and monotonous.

"If I'd say no just because I don't want to do it, I'd feel unbearably guilty."

"I'd get fired if I spoke up about the discrimination practiced against two minority men at the plant."

"If I told my husband how much I resent his silent treatment, he'd never talk to me again."

"I don't think there's any use to try. Nobody listens to me anyway."

"I know better than to open my mouth about anything. I'd only be asking for trouble."

"I'm with Lincoln, who said, 'Better to remain silent and be thought a fool than to speak out and remove all doubt.'"

The common threads running through each of these are a similar seed of powerlessness and a characteristic pessimism about the worth of self and of others.

When worth can be affirmed and power asserted, self-esteem is enhanced in the actor and modeled for those around him or her.

To be affirmative of the worth of persons and assertive for human rights is to unite the two sides of effective relationships into personal wholeness. This involves knowing your personal rights while respecting equally the rights of others; doing something about your potentials while encouraging equally the realization of others' capabilities.

Translated to the simplest human relationships, it means saying "I love you" as well as "I'm asking from you." It means communicating "I want to be with you" as clearly as "I want something from you." It means communicating caring as unmistakably as any requesting.

"I really care about Jean," Jim tells me. "I'm sure she has no idea. We worked together for a summer internship. Now she's away in California, and I'm here in graduate school, so there's nothing I can do."

"Have you considered Ma Bell as an instant go-between?"

"Oh, I'd call if I knew Jean's number. But then, what could I say?"

"How about, 'Hi, Jean. This is Jim. I've been thinking about you a lot. I miss you very much; I want you to know. I'd love to see you again, soon. Now that I hear your voice I'm realizing how much I really do care!'"

"I can't say anything like that. I'd say, 'Hi, Jean. This is Jim. Just wanted to call. How are you?' Then I'm stuck."

"To say 'I care' is a gift worth giving."

"Yes, but it's a risky gift, and she might refuse it. I want friendship with her so much, yet I'm afraid she'll reject me."

"But if you never tell her you care, you both lose. To affirm you care is to admit you do appreciate her, whether she wants to pursue the relationship or not. To assert that you want friendship is to declare what you feel. You've lost nothing if you call."

"You're right. I can be more assertive. And affirmative. I'll try information. Tonight. I'll bet I can reach her!"

"By phone, you mean?"

"Yeh, by phone, and by heart too!"

Asserting *and* affirming is the key to strong and close relationships. Assertiveness skills can equip you to stand up for what you value and want. Affirmative skills can free you to stand with the other as you express your needs and your wants so you can seek a solution satisfying to both of you! Having the courage to stand up and the caring to stand with, both at the same time without one diminishing the other, is a skill to be learned and a gift to be received.

To truly value both yourself and your fellows—equally—is a gift of love you can accept for yourself and then offer equally to others. The chapter on loving skills will aid you in working at giving and receiving love.

To be clearly assertive in claiming your needs and wants without aggressively intruding into another's domain or violating the other's dignity is a skill to be learned. The chapters on living skills will provide insight for your growth and exercises for your experiencing of alternate ways of asserting your power as a person and responding to others' assertiveness.

To blend both sides of yourself—your asserting and affirming halves—into an integrated lifestyle is the first crucial step toward wholeness. The chapter on Loving *and* Living Skills will provide models for bringing both together without sacrificing either. As assertive skills are expressed in affirmative styles, positive living results.

Exercises on Passive Excuses

Perhaps the preceding chapter has evoked a few of your favorite reasons for using nonassertive and nonaffirmative behavior. The following short course on expert excuse-making is offered to support your objections to assertive and affirmative behavior when someone is taking advantage of or imposing on you.

1. "Well, it's just this one time; I can take it. I'll just overlook the inconvenience and consider the source." (Since this situation will be over in a moment, I may never see this person again, I can easily overlook it. Why should I care about my self-esteem? What's one more embarrassing failure? If I let the other impose on me, what does it hurt if I encourage such behavior in others?)

2. "I don't want to raise a fuss; the last thing I want is to make a scene. I'll go along with it." (Clear assertiveness exercised in an affirmative way might change the inconvenience or the injustice quickly; but someone might be watching or the other person may be offended, and I hope to live my whole life without either offending anyone or even inconveniencing a soul.)

3. "No one else has complained about the service; it must be acceptable to others. Maybe I'm too sensitive." (If you complain, the businessman will likely reassure you that you are the very first, and everyone else seems to like his services. Don't challenge him, since you are obviously in the wrong. Conclude that you are the oddball who is overreacting. Dummy up!)

4. "I'll get labeled as a troublemaker. I hate it when others call me names or label my behavior." (If others call me a name, it hurts me, not them. If they label me, I'm found out, I'm embarrassed, I feel put down. I'm powerless to point out that their labels are their expressions of their own problems.)

5. "I don't want to make something big out of nothing; I'd just be blowing it all out of proportion." (I can explain away the conflict for the time being. If I resent it later on, I can deal with that then. I can't talk back, or the situation will always turn into something worse.)

6. "I can just be big about it. I'll act as if it's nothing. I'll do the excusing for the other person." (I can make up excuses for other's behavior—like, "he didn't really mean it," "he was upset and not really himself." I can make allowance for others no matter how much it inconveniences me or invites them to continue coercing and controlling others.)

If you are affirmatively assertive, you know that immediate, firm, gentle, and nondefensive statements of what you want can break through cycles of put-downs or cut through situations in which you are being put upon. You act justly. You ask for just responses.

Experiencing Asserting and Affirming

Reflect on a recent conflict with a close friend. Focus on the key issues at stake in the conflict. Define what you really wanted, and what the other wanted. Recall what assumptions you held about the relationship. How much do you care about the other person? Did you express it in words? In tone of voice? In actions? List your responses:

Affirmation	*but/and*	*Assertion*
I care about you _____		I need from you _____
_____		_____
I value your _____		I want from you _____
_____		_____
I prize your _____		I expect you to _____
_____		_____

1. When you have filled out three answers to each of the above, read them aloud, affirmation followed by assertion, with the conjunction *but*. Feel the impact of presenting your case with the affirmation and the assertion placed in contradiction. *But* is not conjunctive; it is disjunctive. It separates, splits, creates tension in self and others.

2. Speak them aloud with the connecting word *and*. Feel the integrative and conjunctive message. Practice the behavior with the other person and invite his or her feedback on the difference in expressing "both-and" instead of saying "I care-but-I want."

3. Rehearse a situation that you need to negotiate soon and express it in assert-and-affirm words. Write out your script for expressing both loving and leveling (the latter meaning to be assertive and forthright about your needs and feelings).

Chapter 2.

ASSERTIVENESS
The Uses of Power

"What shall I do?" Pauline asks. "I can't trust my husband another day. I have enough evidence to convict a saint.

"First, I have this bill from a hotel in the Poconos for two guests, signed with my husband's signature. I've never been to the Poconos. Then I have a room key for a motel that I found in my husband's drawer. I've never been near that motel. Obviously he has!

"Last week when I was visiting my mother in Chicago, I called home at 8:00 A.M. A sweet feminine voice answered the phone. He had a woman there at eight in the morning! I hung up without a word. What more do I need to prove that he's playing around?"

Three strikes, and he's obviously out, if Pauline will choose to use the evidence to establish guilt.

If Pauline plays passive, she may just save her stockpile of nuclear-family explosives until the suspected skirt-chaser trips himself up. Saving up her wrath until he brings the world down on his own head may release her from the responsibility of triggering the showdown, but it also requires that Pauline betray her own dignity, silence her own integrity, stifle her true feelings. The cost of playing passive to keep peace is incredibly high.

If Pauline chooses to take aggressive action, she may throw the evidence in his face, charging, trying, convicting, and sentencing him in one furious rage. If words—blaming, labeling, judging, condemning words—fail her, she can act out her anger in more volatile or violent ways.

However, when the smoke clears, the embattled husband may get his chance for equal time. The bill from the Poconos hotel is from the forgotten ski trip dad and son took last January. The motel key was left in the guest room by a visiting friend who had carried it off forgetfully and left it in the bureau drawer. The early morning feminine voice? Just a babysitter who came in early so the kids wouldn't be alone while dad was off to a 6:00 A.M. business breakfast.

Having rushed to judgment, Pauline is, at best, in an awkward position. By assuming an attitude of suspicion, she has seriously reduced the basic trust level between herself and her husband.

An assertive Pauline could report what she is confused about as soon as it occurs. "I'm puzzled by this bill, dear. I don't recall what the Pocono trip was about," or, "I just found this key to a strange motel. I'm wondering how it wound up in our house?"

No accusations, no blaming, no aggressive attack. Pauline is simply asserting her curiosity. If she affirms respect for her husband's point of view at the same time, she can build trust even as she checks out what's puzzling her.

To react too strongly—aggressively—or to respond too weakly—passively—either is generally ineffective. The median point—assertiveness—is the point of balance that allows the actor all the needed strength but without the pain of overreacting in stress or overstating the case in defense or offense.

The Nonassertive Response

Passive persons give away their power to those around them by responding to others in weaker than appropriate ways. Playing nonassertive may be motivated by the need to be nice or to present a socially acceptable face. "Peace at any price" is the goal; "nice at any cost" is the way to reach it.

Gene Genial, for example, is one of the nicest guys I know, but his niceness creates the usual corrosive side effects of dishonesty, distance, denial, and danger which seem to inevitably accompany nice-guyness.

Gene genially accepts any and all criticism from others with niceness and passive warmth. This creates an atmosphere of sweetness and superficiality that stifles others' frankness and discourages them from giving him genuine honest feedback on his behavior. So he lives in a world of dishonesty.

Gene is much too genial and gentle to give others level, honest feedback on their behavior. This encourages others to sit on their negative feelings and tends to force them to turn their frustration inward against themselves, generating resentment, guilt, and depression. So he lives in a world of denial.

Gene is afraid of open conflict and uses nonassertive niceness to keep away from any open hassles with others. Thus they are never sure if the relationship could survive an angry interchange if it occurred, so they too must be ever on guard. So he lives in a world of safe distance.

Gene is genial on the surface, but inside the accumulated frustration churns his emotional (and sometimes his physical) stomach. When he gets overloaded, he is likely to feel explosive. Such rage eruptions may occur unexpectedly over a small issue when others are unprepared. In addition, the stress takes its toll on his bodily functions, creating unease and disease. It's not nice to play nice. Being nonassertive is costly in dishonest, denied, distant, and dangerous relationships.

The nonassertive person has a tendency to deny his or her own worth and value as a human being.

Gene Genial, behaving in kind nonassertiveness, allows others to walk over him, exploit him, and use him to their advantage and to his disadvantage. He seldom stands up for the privileges that are his as a human being. He does not expect to be respected and related to as a person who is equal in worth to any other person. Gene's nonassertive behavior is also a way of avoiding threat. Since he is often used and exploited, he has reason to avoid close relationships to keep from getting hurt. He avoids dealing with problems in relationships because so frequently he comes out on the bottom as the person who gets the "raw end" of the deal.

Nonassertive behavior is escape behavior. As shown in the following diagram, when the nonassertive person faces a problem, he does an instant about-face and tries to escape in a nonassertive way. Maintaining the hope that all problems eventually dissolve, he evades them rather than seeking to resolve them. Unsolved difficulties accumulate in his emotional museum and scare him (condition him) to fear the next situation even more.

Nonassertive Behavior	Assertive Behavior	Aggressive Behavior
I have no power to change the situation. (Besides, I'm not worth much anyway.)		
I have no right to protest injustice. I'm helpless. (Besides, I have no right to speak up.)		
I am not responsible for the situation. I must avoid, escape, deny it. It's hopeless. (Besides, things don't change; nothing can be done anyway.)		

The nonassertive person leaves problems hanging unresolved and in an internal limbo. A problem in limbo does not go away. An internal problem becomes an eternal problem. In fact, additional problems accumulate and situations get more complex. It takes two persons to have a problem. Problems are interpersonal. When a person internalizes problems in a passive way, they convert to intrapersonal problems, that is, problems within the self. These conflicts within the self create painful emotional reactions.

Problems within originate in problems without. When old escape behavior blocks us from resolving our problems in living, frustration, tension, anxiety, fear, anger, depression, and so on result. These internal problems began in painful external situations. The "problem" inside a person is a complicated version of the problems outside a person that have been swallowed whole in an indigestible state. The nonassertive person tries to stomach all the difficulties and finds it not only hard to swallow, but hard to keep down. The nonassertive person is frequently subject to explosive temper or impulsive outbursts. Having overcontained stress and overcontrolled frustrations, the toleration levels are reached, and the behavior swings from nonassertive all the way across to aggressive ventilating or acting out.

These aggressive outbursts are unchanneled, so they seldom produce any desirable results. They are uncontrolled, so they often create injurious relationships which are so painful that the nonassertive person retreats in dismay to the old nice-at-any-price position. This reaction only insures that more frustration will accumulate until the explosive point is reached again.

The Aggressive Response

Aggressive behaviors develop in at least two ways. The most common is the explosion of overcontrolled, nonassertive behavior. In this situation a Gene Genial is nonassertive until frustration has accumulated to his limit of tolerance, at which point he blows through his peace-ceiling in unchanneled aggression. The second way aggressive behavior develops is by previous learning and conditioning. In this situation a nonassertive person repeatedly exceeds his limit of tolerance and frequently resorts to aggressive behavior. After a number of such experiences, he grows accustomed to his rage as a habitual response to frustration. All that is then required is the presence of old stimuli (to which he had previously been nonassertive). Now he instantly exceeds his limit of tolerance. After a history of such learning experiences, he no longer responds with the old nonassertive behavior but when presented with negative stimuli, has an

Nonassertive Behavior	Assertive Behavior	Aggressive Behavior
I have no power to change the situation. (Besides, I'm not worth much anyway.)		I am all-powerful and can change situations by force. (Besides, you need my wisdom to know what is best for you anyway.)
I have no right to protest injustice. I'm helpless. (Besides, I have no right to speak up.)		I know "might makes right," and I have both might and right to demand instant change. (Besides, you need me to set you straight anyway.)
I am not responsible for the situation. I must avoid, escape, deny it. It's hopeless. (Besides, things don't change; nothing can be done anyway.)		I cannot tolerate your behavior. You are responsible for my feelings, my pain, my disgust. (Besides, you must change, since you're the one in the wrong anyway.)

immediate aggressive response. For example, if a teenager and his parent are repeatedly in conflict, just being in each other's presence is sufficient stimulus to trigger aggressive behavior.

Aggressive behavior is demand behavior. It assumes inappropriate power, takes unjustified action, and exercises inconsiderate coercion.

Aggressive responses abuse power. On the freeway, the aggressive driver in the red Corvette Stingray knifes through three lanes of traffic, pressing for every advantage, cutting in just as the other driver's reflexes relax for a few seconds.

The nonassertive driver in the blue compact who was just cut off and squeezed onto the shoulder through two potholes is sweating profusely. His knuckles clutch the steering wheel whitely. He's wanting to park it, and he's feeling guilty for the impulsive thought of ramming the Corvette up the exit ramp.

In aggressive behavior, the aggressor attempts to enhance himself at the expense of the other. He tries to make himself look better by defacing the other, to elevate himself by bringing the other down to his level. In so doing, he does not improve himself; he deludes himself. Bringing another down does not help me up. The aggressive person takes no risks. By rushing to judgment and vengeance he says, "I will strike before he strikes me." However, in hurting the other person, he is in fact hurting himself. He may rationalize brilliantly and offer excuses eloquently. Precisely because he hurts, he attempts to ease the pain by justifying his behavior. He feels guilty, his conscience confronts him, and he immediately rationalizes the hurt away. This response of guilt or guilty conscience is an extremely important response and is necessary for society to survive. If people had no sense of guilt or conscience, aggressive behavior would go uncontrolled in society and humans would destroy themselves. A person who has no sense of guilt over hurting another is said to be a sociopath. Society builds such institutions as prisons to restrict this type of person and protect people from violent and destructive behavior.

Contemporary armamenta of war exaggerate this situation. Atomic and hydrogen bombs can be exploded impersonally thousands of miles from the point of origin at the touch of a button. When aggressive behavior is no longer personalized, the sense of guilt that restrains this type of behavior is weakened. The fear that humankind may destroy itself should concern us. Responsibility for self and with others must be sustained. Aggression dare not be depersonalized. Guilt is necessary, valuable, and must be realistically maintained for effective control of aggressive and destructive behavior.

Not only does the aggressive person hurt when he strikes out, because he injures someone else of equal value to himself; but the other person, likewise human, becomes instantly defensive and almost invariably strikes back and hurts the aggressive person a second time. Ironically, the aggressive person who attempts to escape from the vulnerability and risk creates a system that hurts him not once but twice or more every time he inflicts hurt on another. This is the paradox of aggressive behavior. Whereas the aggressor attempts to avoid risk, protect himself, or save his life, he in fact exaggerates risk, hurts himself, and is in greater danger of his life. In contrast, the assertive person who is willing to take the risk of vulnerability frequently enriches his life relationships and preserves the dignity and trust that is the heart of life itself.

Since life has meaning and fulfillment only in mutually rewarding and satisfying interpersonal relationships, the aggressive person has effectively destroyed his or her life. By striking out at others, he or she causes others to withdraw behind protective walls that preserve safe existence. Consequently, the aggressive person is left lonely, isolated, and outside intimate relationships.

The aggressive person may turn the anger inward and strike back at himself. Aggression inevitably boomerangs. When one inverts it and makes the self the target he is only rushing to judgment in condemning himself, denigrating his worth, comparing the self unfavorably with others, and progressively considers himself unworthy of other people's care and concern. Withdrawal, distancing, wall-building, isolation from interpersonal relationships results. Thus he loses real life because he has successfully destroyed his relationships.

The ultimate end result of striking-out behavior is murder; the ultimate conclusion of striking back at oneself is suicide. In between these tragic extremes of aggressive behavior is the broad spectrum of destructive relationships that corrode community.

Study the diagram on the next page carefully to visualize how both nonassertive and aggressive behavior can be used to attack others or to injure the self.

DOWN ON OTHERS			ATTACKING OTHERS
	Yield to win by guilt Doormat behavior Service, acquiescence	Ultimate extreme: murder Driving others away Striking at others	
	⇧	⇧	
	Self-sacrifice	Other-attack	
	⇧	⇧	

	Nonassertive	Assertive	Aggressive

DOWN ON SELF			ATTACKING SELF
	⇩	⇩	
	Self-stagnation	Self-attack	
	⇩	⇩	
	Apathy, helplessness Hopelessness Depression	Striking at self in isolation Withdrawal Ultimate extreme: suicide	

The items above the center line show what happens when the nonassertive or aggressive behavior is turned outward against others. The items beneath the line describe the effect of turning aggressive or nonassertive responses inward against the self. The tragic end of such behavior is depression and slow destruction of self.

Assertive behavior which prizes both self and others refuses such self-sacrifice or self-destructiveness; it rejects any strategies of attacking self or others. As one recognizes and comes to realize in daily relationship the equal worth and preciousness of both self and others, true assertiveness frees persons to live in healthful ways.

Medicine is becoming more and more aware of the emotional aspects of physical diseases. It seems there are few major diseases that do not have an emotional component. We know that such diseases as asthma, high blood pressure, heart attacks, ulcers, colitis, and even diabetes are strongly suspect as having an emotional component. Under adequate emotional stress, the physical body will respond and the weakest link in the body will break. Whatever disease that link represents will be manifested. A great many of us may die of diseases many years sooner than we would need to if our behavior allowed our interpersonal relationships to be more meaningful and fulfilling. Assertive behavior offers the best potential for such a life. The next several chapters of this book will present some guidelines for learning and utilizing assertive behavior more effectively.

The Assertive Response

Assertive behavior is problem-solving behavior. The assertive person sees the conflict, recognizes its true importance, and seeks a solution satisfactory to both self and others.

Fleeing the problem (nonassertively) by use of denial or distancing is futile. Fighting (aggressively) is a false solution, since force only increases the hurt and invites counterforce. Facing the differences (assertively) and working toward a mutually desirable outcome frees both persons in an interpersonal problem situation to experience their worth, their power, and their dignity.

The assertive person may not have the necessary data at his or her fingertips to resolve the problem at the moment it occurs. He or she may file the problem for the time being until it is possible to gather more information and then return to finish it. More time may be required to reflect and understand the situation so negotiation is postponed until he or she has a sense of insight to contribute to the solution. Yet there is no avoidance. Commitment to assertively achieve a mutual conciliation is not in question.

Assertive, appropriate, person-enhancing behavior is its own reward. It is self-reinforcing. To act assertively is to act effectively and this is to act confidently, powerfully, responsibly. The self-enhancement of using power justly is deeply satisfying.

Nonassertive Behavior	Assertive Behavior	Aggressive Behavior
I have no power to change the situation. (Besides, I'm not worth much anyway.)	I have equal power with others. I can change my position toward a conflict, my behaviors toward others, my responses to their words and actions.	I am all powerful and can change situations by force. (Besides, you need my wisdom to know what is best for you anyway.)
I have no right to protest injustice. I'm helpless. (Besides, I have no right to speak up.)	I have equal rights with others. I can protest injustice; I can assert my needs for honest, fair, and equal relationships.	I know "might makes right," and I have both might and right to demand instant change. (Besides, you need me to set you straight anyway.)
I am not responsible for the situation, I must avoid, escape, deny it. It's hopeless. (Besides, things don't change; nothing can be done anyway.)	I am responsible for the thoughts I think, the words I speak, the actions I take. I am always responsible; I am never to blame.	I cannot tolerate your behavior. You are responsible for my feelings, my pain, my disgust. (Besides, you must change, since you're the one in the wrong anyway.

Assertive responses come from a balanced sense of shared power, equal power with the other, equal ability to work through differences, equal responsibility to reach clear and comfortable responsibility with each other. Thus, assertive behavior is appropriate to the situation. No two situations are truly alike, and they are constantly changing, rapidly rearranging themselves. A person's behavior changes slowly, and what is appropriate today must be examined carefully tomorrow. Consequently the assertive person is continually reevaluating his or her behavior as well as reassessing the situation to be certain the behavior is appropriate to person, place, and purpose.

Assertive behavior enhances relationships, enhances the worth of self, enhances the value of the other. If both people are assertive, the resulting impact of a disagreement will be the mutual discovery that both will be feeling better about each other and about themselves. It is affirming behavior. Each affirms both self and other, both self-worth and the preciousness of the other human being.

Assertive behavior is vulnerable or risk-taking behavior. When the assertive person reaches out to the other person, he makes himself vulnerable to that person. He takes the risk of being rejected or ignored or physically hurt. That result, however, is rather infrequent. Usually when the assertive person reaches out in an assertive, enhancing way, he gets a positive response from the recipient. He may receive nine positive responses out of ten or he may receive ninety-nine out of a hundred, but once in a while someone will strike back in some form. This is the risk the assertive person takes. However, he sees it as a risk worth taking. The odds are good and the assertive person has learned that the long-term consequences of assertiveness are invariably more rewarding than the long-term consequences of nonassertive behavior. He will, therefore, accept the risk because on the long-term basis assertive behavior results in the warm, fulfilling, and deep relationships which most of us desire.

Thus the assertive person is regularly reinforced for his positive behavior by achieving successful relationships. But the negative feedback is also a strong factor to be considered since occasionally—"intermittently," we say—there is negative reinforcement from nonassertive or aggressive responses given by others. The temptation to slip back into a passive response or to slap back with an aggressive response can be great. Clear awareness of the ineffectiveness of old nonassertive and aggressive behaviors can help reduce the temptation. Clear recall of the rewards of assertive effectiveness can induce the determination to remain assertive. Gradually, the power of assertive and affirmative living becomes its own reward.

Nonassertive Behavior	Assertive Behavior	Aggressive Behavior
	A. Problem-solving behavior B. Appropriate behavior C. Growth-enhancing behavior for worth of both self and others D. Vulnerable behavior (risk-taking behavior)	
	When the assertive person reaches out to the other person, there is the risk of being rejected, or hurt . . .	
If the other withdraws, sulks, pouts, rejects passively	he is not hurt every time; his trust is not betrayed each time (maybe once in ten times—1:10—or once in a hundred—1:100).	If the other attacks with verbal or physical hostility
Negative passive feedback		Negative active feedback
	The temptation is . . .	
To slip back to nonassertiveness		To slap back to aggressiveness

Experiencing Assertiveness

Read the following situations; formulate your own assertive response. Then identify the following six as
nonassertive, assertive, or aggressive.

1. You are riding in the front seat beside the driver,
stopped at a red light, first in line in heavy traffic. The light
changes and the driver makes no move to go. You say:

_____ a. "What on earth are you waiting for?
Have you decided to spend the night
here?"

_____ b. "Dear, . . . do you think maybe . . . ?
Oh, never mind."

_____ c. "The light's green."

_____ d. "Where in the blazes is your head?
You must be wool-gathering in the
clouds somewhere."

_____ e. "Look, dear, the light is exactly the
same shade as my dress."

_____ f. "Why don't you let me drive, you
absent-minded clown? After all, you
had the last two wrecks."

2. You are waiting in line at the supermarket when a large
arrogant-appearing person cuts into the line in front of you.
Your response:

_____ a. "Can't you see we're standing in line?
Who gave you permission to butt in?
Butt out!"

_____ b. You say nothing, but clear your throat sharply and look away, avoiding the line-crasher's eyes.

_____ c. "Sir, I've been waiting in line four minutes, and you have just taken my place. Please respect the rights of those waiting their turn."

_____ d. "Clerk, this person just crashed the line. Can you ask the manager to come up here?"

_____ e. You say, "Pardon me," and elbow past the person, to stand squarely in front of him or her, keeping your back turned.

_____ f. "Perhaps you didn't notice there is a line waiting. These five people were here before you."

3. You are sitting in the back of the classroom as the teacher is giving assignments for class projects and calling only on volunteers in the front rows. You want equal opportunity at the choice projects, but are unable to get her attention. Your response:

_____ a. You give up in disgust and sit on your hands, knowing she will not recognize your hand anyway.

_____ b. You yell, "Unfair, unfair," and then tell her in no uncertain terms that the way she is running the class assignments is—

_____ c. You get up and leave, doubting whether you will go back, considering writing an anonymous letter of criticism to her and to the principal.

_____ d. You stand until you have her attention, and say, "Ms. Brown, I would like equal opportunity for me and for others in the back of the room to make selections. Could you use another process?"

_____ e. You start complaining loudly to fellow seatmates about her incompetence. Your sarcastic remarks stimulate laughter and disrupt the session.

_____ f. You sit quietly, slowly building anger; then as class is dismissed, you can hold it in no longer, so you give the teacher a verbal jibe as you pass: "You always give the people in front first chance at everything."

Our point of view—

Of course, an exaggerated tone of voice, body posture, or facial signals can turn an assertive response into an aggressive attack, but all things being equal we rate the above as:

1. Nonassertive, b and e; assertive, c; aggressive, a, d, f.
2. Nonassertive, b; assertive, c, f; aggressive, a, d, e.
3. Nonassertive, a, c; assertive, d; aggressive, b, e; nonassertive followed by an aggressive explosion, f.

Chapter 3.

AFFIRMATION
The Ways of Love

"I'm really afraid of that man," Dan tells me. He's biting his lip. He's minister of a prominent church. And he's afraid of his associate pastor.

"The man is out to ruin me. He's circulating rumors that have just a little bit of truth in them, enough to make them dangerous, and a whole lot of lie. If I fight him, people will believe the stories are true the moment I start my defense. If I ignore him, the tales will keep growing. I'm damned if I do, damned if I don't. And, worst of all, I can't talk to the man."

"What have you tried?"

"Well, I asked for his loyalty and support as an associate. He promised me that. Then I demanded he silence the rumors he started. He denied it all. Then I threatened to have him fired by the board. And he said, 'We'll see who gets fired!' He's been working underhandedly against me ever since."

"So you tried a superficial agreement. When that failed you used threats, and now you're trying a power squeeze. You've found three things that don't work."

"So what else is there? I care about the man. I like him as an associate. And I want to have a clear agreement to trust each other. I value honesty. I need his assistance on the pastoral team. If I could only tell him both things at the same time—"

Dan is in real trouble. He cares about the relationship with his associate, and he cares about him as a person. Somehow he's incapable of expressing it. He is nonassertive in working through issues of disagreement, and he is nonaffirmative in expressing how he values the other's work, performance, team relationships, and his dignity as a human being.

Dan needs both affirmation and assertion skills to enable him to live effectively in tense relationships.

The Nonaffirmative Response

"I'm fed up with your going on a wild spending spree and blowing your whole budget," Ann says, stabbing at Ralph angrily with a blaming finger. "You get carried away with optimism and blow the whole next month's income." Ralph refuses to acknowledge her words, her blaming, her presence. Each is invalidating the other, ignoring each other to cancel out the pain of contact. No affirmation is heard from either; neither offers it in return. Stalemate!

Nonaffirmative responses to others can be expressed in a whole spectrum of styles, from passive avoidance of all recognition of the other's presence to an active use of abrasive words or abusive acts. Love can be silently withheld or verbally negated in criticism, sarcasm, clever innuendo.

The most common violence is bitter silence. To ignore another's presence, or to refuse to acknowledge his or her worth and significance, can be an invitation to die. Nonaffirming responses withhold the emotional support that nourishes relationship and withdraw the most elemental tokens of acceptance. No words, no touch, no eye contact, no signal recognize the other's presence, reveal awareness that the other exists!

"The bum. I befriended my neighbor woman—she had no friends at all, including her husband—and then she had the gall to steal my husband. He's a bum, a tramp, a no-goodnik."

She sits, her cold shoulder turned toward him. She has not looked directly at him since arriving in my office, and she speaks only in third person, as though he were absent. She refuses to be present.

Simple presence is the most fundamental form of nonverbal recognition and communication between persons. It is the elemental language of relationship, the chief means of granting or withholding approval, recognition, and validation of others. Presence is the essence of caring and love. It is the prime indication of who is viewed as important by whom. It involves doing and saying very little. The power and effectiveness lie in what we convey through attention and awareness. The art of presence is simply "being there" for another in a genuine, caring, receptive, accepting frame of mind.

Refusing to be present is a common nonaffirming behavior used by both passive and aggressive persons. Withdrawal in nonassertive silence and avoidance may be acted out in a refusal to be present. Rejection in aggressive blaming or hostile distancing is also a flight from presence. Nothing renders human interaction more impotent than nonaffirmative behaviors.

Nonaffirming relationships are often learned as a response to fear. "You might reject me, so I'll reject you." "You do not respect me. Why should I respect you?" "You might take advantage of me, insult me, scorn me, so I'll keep my distance from you."

Nonaffirming Behavior	Affirming Behavior	Absorbing Behavior
I care little about you. (I've more than enough difficulty looking out for me.)		
I can't reach out in respect or appreciation. (I need to be loved before I have any love to offer.)		
If I never open myself to loving relationships, I am safe from being hurt. (If I risk nothing, I lose nothing.)		

Nonaffirming signals stimulate identical behavior in others (which becomes a similar stimulus in turn). Unloving actions trigger unloving reactions in an accelerating spiral. Negative behaviors tend to snowball. Like self-fulfilling prophecy, the nonaffirming response creates nonaffirming relationships that culminate in resentment and rejection.

"I thought I liked Linda when we began dating, but the last six months have been hopeless. I don't know why I keep going back for more of the criticisms and putdowns she keeps laying on me," Chuck says. "Maybe it's because there are some really beautiful moments, although they're so few and far between. That's what behaviorists call intermittent reinforcement," he says, grinning. "It's the most powerful kind. Seems like I'll put up with all kinds of hassling because I've got this hope that in five minutes she'll come through with a little caring and respect."

Having heard himself spell it out, Chuck's eyes widen; he's shaking his head vigorously. "That's it. That's it. She's my mother all over again. Negative, negative, negative; a quick touch of appreciation, then back to the stream of negatives. She has my dad eating out of her hand. That's what I'm doing to Linda. Except I'm also biting the hand that intermittently feeds me. I'm doing the negative stuff too. We're just no good for each other."

Nonaffirming behavior is sterile. It can create nothing when silent and passive. It is extinction behavior. It says, "Cease and desist." When focused consistently on a particular behavior, it frequently can reduce it to extinction in short order. When active and verbal, it is negative or punitive behavior that frequently stimulates like response, or more intense negative responses in others. Either way, it is uncreative, nonproductive, self-defeating, and self-destructing.

The pain of rejection, the fear of being devalued, is so intense that nonaffirming persons often swing to the opposite extreme in seeking to be absorbed in another (total safety in being swallowed up by a loving other) or to absorb another so he or she is powerless to reject (total security in incorporating the love object).

Like the nonassertive person who overloads with anger

and erupts with an aggressive response, the nonaffirming person becomes overcharged with fear and flees into absorption as the absorber or the absorbed.

The Absorbing Response

"All I want is to live for my husband and son," Mamie says, with deep emotion. "They are my whole life. My only reason for living is to make them happy. That's all I want. Now if that's not loving, what is it?"

Absorption. Not love. It's absorbing and being absorbed. It's the stickiest, most seductive, most dangerous response. Trying to negotiate with an absorber is like boxing with a sticky pest-strip. Your punches are not only absorbed, so are you. Flypaper love clings, then collects the "beloved" until the oneness becomes permanent attachment.

More of a good thing is seldom better. Salt is good. More salt becomes astringent; too much salt is toxic, even lethal. Affection is joy in closeness to another. More affection is infatuation, which makes life without the beloved intolerable; still more affection becomes obsession in which one or both selves are swallowed up in the other.

Selfhood is destroyed equally as much by absorption as by aggression. Children are equally impaired by a parent absorbing them into emotional fusion as by rejection and emotional exclusion.

The sins committed in "love" are more diabolical than those driven by hate. Hate at least sees the hated as an "other," as a person worthy of address, or even attack. Absorption sees self and other as one and consumes the other self with undisturbed conscience.

A husband may "helpfully" absorb his wife into his own dream, his own work, his own lifestyle. She may sacrifice her selfhood in being absorbed, and slowly atrophy as a person.

A mother may "lovingly" care for a special child with absorbing concern. Slowly the child is incorporated and gradually impaired. The sense of emerging selfhood is stifled and often permanently stunted.

Absorption has as many forms as there are fears, as many faces as there are needs for fusion security. Absorption is an exaggeration of loving intimacy; it is not loving integrity. As a gross caricature of love, it pretends to have the best interests of the other at heart. In reality, its own definition of what is good for the other gets imposed on the other.

"I wanted dancing lessons so badly when I was a girl, but my dad made fun of me and my mother called it a waste of good money. I promised myself my daughter would get what I never had. And she is! Is she grateful? No way!"

The mother is loving her daughter as she (the mother) wants to be loved. Beautiful! Except for one major thing. She hasn't asked how the daughter wants to be loved. Does she want dancing lessons? Not on your life! She loves horses and wants to take riding lessons. But mother loves her too much to allow her to settle for what is obviously (to mother) second best. So the pressure, the guilt, the controls, the

Nonaffirming Response	Affirming Response	Absorbing Response
I care little about you. (I've more than enough difficulty looking out for me.)		I care only about you. (I live only to make you happy. I want only the best for you.)
I can't reach out in respect or appreciation. (I need to be loved before I have any love to offer.)		I willingly and totally sacrifice myself for your sake. (You should be grateful that I never try to make you feel grateful.)
If I never open myself to loving relationships, I am safe from being hurt. (If I risk nothing, I lose nothing.)		I know what is best for you. I love you too much to give you less. (If I control you, it is only for your own good.)

denial, the false niceness, the daughter's lonely sadness all cement the absorbing unity of mother and daughter.

The Affirming Response

Authentic loving relationships are identified by the equal affirmation given to both self and other. The affirmative person can stand firm in awareness of his or her own value and hold firmly to the other's equal value.

To be affirmative is to see the worth of the other even as we see our own, to prize the other's freedom and fulfillment as we do our own.

Impact in resolving conflict is largely the exercise of skills in being firmly affirmative. To care for the other's satisfaction as we do our own is to seek solutions satisfying to both parties in a hassle. To care about the other's point of view is to define the conflict neutrally, narrowly, mutually in a way that frees both persons to win—in a win-win solution, not a win-lose.

Affirmative responses reach out to stand with the other person even as we are focusing on the different points of view we stand for. To have someone to stand with and something to stand for expresses our wholeness as a person and invites the other to be truly completely present.

Affirmation is to love what assertion is to power. Affirmation lets love find its balance of equality, gives love its practice of mutuality, invites love to create relationships of reciprocity.

Affirmation expresses equality.

Love is not the benevolence of a superior person being kind to an inferior. "I can love another even though he is unlovable or she is unlovely." Such an unequal love belittles the beloved in the very definition.

Love is not self-sacrificial service—not essentially. Love may choose to serve in a self-sacrificing way, but not all self-sacrifice is loving; some is unbearably self-righteous and designed to control and motivate another by guilt.

Love is not simply obedience to an ideal, or a universal human or moral good. To know that another loves us because they "have to, should, or ought" provides little joy or support.

Nonaffirming Response	Affirming Response	Absorbing Response
I care little about you. (I've more than enough difficulty looking out for me.)	I care for you as for myself. My freedom to be me and your freedom to be you are equally worthful.	I care only about you. (I love only to make you happy. I want only the best for you.)
I can't reach out in respect or apprecia-tion. (I need to be loved before I have any love to offer.)	I prize you as I prize myself. I am worthful as I am, not as I act. I am always responsible for my behavior, but never to blame.	I willingly and to-tally sacrifice myself for your sake. (You should be grateful that I never try to make you feel grate-ful.)
If I never open my-self to loving rela-tionships, I am safe from being hurt. (If I risk nothing, I lose nothing.)	I will value you as I value myself. I will seek to hear, honor, and trust you with equal regard. I will be open to seek rela-tionships satisfying to us both.	I know what is best for you. I love you too much to give you less. (If I con-trol you it is only for your own good.)

Affirming love is "equal regard." This definition is the essential definition of love in the Judeo-Christian ethical heritage. It is classically called "agape." Such love prizes the other equally with the self, values the other mutually, and seeks to fulfill itself in open, caring reciprocity. All good relationships are two-way. I affirm your freedom; you affirm mine.

First affirm. Then assert. Then master the art of affirming and asserting simultaneously! This frees us to be authen-tically powerful in relationships since to be truly loving transforms power, and to be truly powerful translates loving into effective living.

Experiencing Affirmation

Read the following situations; formulate your own immediate response in the space provided.

1. Your daughter Cindy is feeling really down. She has
just been cut out of her circle of friends by a teenage hassle
over boyfriends. Jill, one of the other girls, was jilted by her
"steady" who then asked Cindy to the class party. Since she
already had other plans, she is now rejected by her old
friends and didn't gain the new friend either. She wants to
confront them, but is too upset now. Your response:

Now identify the six options that follow as nonaffirmative,
affirmative, or absorbing.

_____ a. "Forget it. A hundred years from
now it won't matter at all."

_____ b. "So what, Cindy? Who needs friends
like them anyway? After all, you've
got your family. Aren't we enough?"

_____ c. "I can hear that it really hurts to get
blamed for what Jim did when you
had no choice in the matter. I think
you'll be able to work it out as the
right time comes."

_____ d. "That's just what you get for being
so friendly and popular. If you
hadn't been flirting with Jim, it
wouldn't have happened."

_____ e. "I'm so fed up with the way that Jill turns the other girls against you when things aren't going her way. I'm going to tell her mother a thing or two when I see her."

_____ f. "I'd be angry too if I were treated like that. I wonder if Jill knows how it really happened or if talking to her would help? If anyone could get through, I would bet on you."

2. You are surprised to discover that Bill, who works beside you every day, is calling for a taxi to take him to the shop where his car is being repaired. You have asked him for favors before; now he won't ask you for such a simple thing as dropping him at the garage. Your response:

_____ a. "What's the big idea calling a taxi, Bill? Ain't I a good enough friend that you can impose on me once in a while?"

_____ b. "Hold it, Bill. Cancel that taxi. I'm driving you over there and I won't take no for an answer and that settles it."

_____ c. "Come on now, Bill. I owe you one and you're not asking me for help? You too good to accept a favor or something?"

_____ d. "Bill, I'll be happy to drive you over. I'd enjoy a few minutes to talk when we're not on the time clock."

_____ e. You say nothing, but conclude to yourself, "Now I know how he feels about favors. I'll never ask for or offer another with him."

_____ f. "Can I help, Bill? I'll be going right by the garage at 5:00. I'd be glad for you to ride with me."

3. Your wife has met you at the door with fire in her eyes. You're an hour late from work. You both are to be at an important dinner date in ten minutes. You'd forgotten all about it. She is apparently really burned at you and is ready to let it all out. Your response:

_____ a. "Don't say a bitchy word. I have my reasons. I'll be ready in no time flat."

_____ b. "I didn't want to go to that dinner anyway, and now that you're up in the air I wish I'd never heard of it."

_____ c. "I'm late. I forgot all about it. I don't blame you for being angry; I would be too. I'll take responsibility for our lateness. I'll be ready in a minute, O.K.?"

_____ d. "O.K., I heard you. So what does a little bit late matter, anyway? Do you have to come on like your mother every time I'm a few minutes behind your precious schedule?"

_____ e. "Look, don't say anything you'll regret or this will be an evening you'll remember for a long time!"

_____ f. "I'm so sorry, dear. I feel so lousy to have messed up your plans. I'll make it up to you some way. I really feel rotten about my running overtime at the job, but I've been overloaded. I'm only doing the overtime for you anyway."

Our point of view—

—is just that, since a sarcastic tone of voice, gesture, facial expression can turn even an "I love you" into a painful dig or jab. But the ratings we give the above are as follows:

1. Nonaffirmative, a and d; affirmative, c and f; absorbing, b and e.
2. Nonaffirmative, a, c, e; affirmative, d and f; absorbing, b.
3. Nonaffirmative, a, b, d, e; affirmative, c; absorbing, f.

Agreed?

Chapter 4.
AND
Joining Love and Power in Personal Wholeness

"I really do love that girl," Dale says, swinging a thumb at his wife, "but I'm fed up. I'm through. I can't take any more."

"Tell her what you just told me," I suggest.

"She knows. She knows. Oh . . . all right. Sue, I've had it with you. I'm ready to call it quits."

"Hey, you missed half of your message. Try again," I insist.

"Oh, I guess I did. . . . o.к. I really do love you, Sue, but when you get to criticizing me, I get so uptight, I want out, like now, right now!"

"I feel both ways about you too," Sue replies. "I really care and I'm really tired of the hassle. I feel both ways most of the time."

"Hm . . . yeah . . . I feel both ways at the same time, too," Dale admits. "I care and I don't care. I want the marriage to work and I want to get away. I'd like for us to be close again, and I'm afraid to try. Somehow it sounds different when I say it that way. I care and I don't care. I want to work it out and I wonder if it's worth it. I guess it's possible to feel both ways at the same time."

"Yes . . . yes, it is. When you say it that way, I feel kind of affirmed even by the things you demand from me. I don't mind hearing you assert what you want. Maybe if we always did both—said both at the same time—maybe we could work through things better?"

"I'd be willing to try it for a while. I'll report what I want in loving you and what I'd like in leveling with you. Agreed?"

"Agreed."

Effective Living Has Two Sides

Be assertive: extend your power.

Be affirmative: express your respect.

Be assertive and affirmative: experience balanced wholeness.

Each side completes the other. Each tempers, fulfills, integrates the other. Be assertive and experience your power in relationships with impact, with solidity.

Be affirmative and express your respect for yourself and your equal respect for the other. Feel the full richness of relationships in which persons are prized and valued.

Be assertive and affirmative in your stance toward others, and strength to love balances your power in living with others.

Authentic asserting is not an exercise in self-serving individualism. Such a use of power cannot vitalize the self when it violates another. Human beings are relational beings. Any act that injures another injures the actor as well. It takes two people to have a problem, because problems are relational, that is, they are tensions between people. Virtually all conflicts within persons—except for organic brain dysfunctions—originate from conflicts between persons. To hope to resolve a conflict or a tension within the self by dumping it on some other self is circular logic that backfires. A behavior returns its own reward in effective living with others or in inevitable pain with others. Any act of individualistic ignoring of another's welfare and happiness will boomerang.

Asserting and Affirming Are One

Wholeness requires the integration of concern to act caringly about others as persons and the ability to act

daringly in being vulnerable with others in personal relationships. Caring is creating trust. Daring is taking risks.
Risk and trust go together in effective living. It is risky to say
clearly what I want in equal fairness and equal respect with
others. I become vulnerable as I take the initiative in
restructuring relationships to make them more just. I am
venturing into new behaviors as I assert what I want and
affirm what I value. I have to trust that you will hear me, be
open to my honesty, be willing to negotiate change, be
equally concerned about our meeting and finding each other
in integrity and intimacy.

To experience equality in relationships with others, I must
embody equality in myself. If I have an equal balance of
worth—affirmation—and power- ^ssertion—within me, I
can more effectively express this balance to you and experience this justice with you.

To visualize how both dimensions of self-expression fit
together, think of setting the assertiveness scale (nonassertive—assertive—aggressive) on a horizontal plane of moving
toward or away from another. Then matrix it with the
affirmation scale (nonaffirming—affirming—absorbing) on
a vertical plane of moving over or under another. These two
measurements combined provide a model for balanced
living that makes it possible to visualize the four major
elements of effective relationships.

In this two-dimensional model, four basic areas of relationship become immediately visible: 1) freedom (I have
equal right); 2) responsibility (we each have equal responsibility with each other); 3) integrity (we each deserve equal
respect); and 4) worth (we can each perceive the other with
equal regard in authentic loving).

Each of these has both an asserting and an affirming side.
To express any of these four in a one-sided way is only
partly effective.

Asserting my rights without affirming your equal rights
deprives us both of a balanced relationship.

Affirming my responsibility without asserting that I am in
no way responsible for your behaviors, words, and emotions
may keep us both trapped in blaming or in clinging
dependency.

AFFIRM
EQUAL REGARD

I love me.
I equally love you.

I know I am worthful
simply as I am.

I know you are valuable
simply as you are.

ASSERT
EQUAL RIGHTS

I prize my rights.
I equally value yours.

My freedom to be me and
your freedom to be you
are equally precious to me.

```
        A
        F
        F
        I
ASSERTING
        M
        I
        N
        G
```

AFFIRM
EQUAL RESPECT

I respect my integrity.
I equally respect yours.

I will honor my wholeness,
my sense of justice,
my concern for right
relationships.

I will equally honor yours.

ASSERT
EQUAL RESPONSIBILITY

I affirm my responsibility.
I am firm in respecting yours.

The words and acts I choose
are mine: for them I am fully
responsible.

The words and acts you use
are yours: for them I am
in no way responsible.

Asserting my high regard for my own worth without affirming my equal regard for yours creates egotism, not the love of prizing us both as valued persons.

Developing a balanced integration of both the affirming and asserting aspects of genuine respect for us each requires caring about the needs of both of us for equal respect, equal responsibility, equal rights, and equal regard.

If I'm angry at you, I'm wanting my rights honored. I may be feeling invaded and violated by your callous inconsiderateness. If I assert my rights without affirming the quality of respect I want, our relationship may collapse. If I assert my responsibility and try to clarify yours without affirming that I see you as equally worthful, our friendship may be impaired. If I am balanced between the two, you may be able to hear both me and the point I'm making.

Asserting and Affirming Are Balancing

Effective balance in walking requires a two-way equilibrium so we will not fall forward or back, or to either side. This is a parable of our existence.

To be balanced in our use of power, we will not fall backwards in the passive powerlessness of being nonassertive. That is letting oneself be bowled over. Nor will we drive forward in overpowering aggression and fall on our faces. We find a balance of power that lets us roll with the punches and be steady on our feet.

To be balanced in our use of affirmation and affection, we will not seek to enfold and absorb people, on the one hand, or to push them away on the other. Both arms can reach out to people. Balance must be maintained on either side, as any cyclist or canoeist can testify, or all is lost.

Walking, running, skiing, or skating all require a blend of these two forces in balance. So does Life. To keep erect requires right relationships with those on either side, and rightful use of power that moves forward without attacking, advances without invading. In affirmation, people tend to become all righthanded, or all left—all-absorbing in their need for dependent relationships, or all nonaffirming in their avoidance and distancing.

BALANCE IS THE KEY

To topple right
is to seize
and to squeeze
too tightly,
to overcontrol,
to absorb

To tip left
is to withdraw
from relationships,
to be nonaffirming

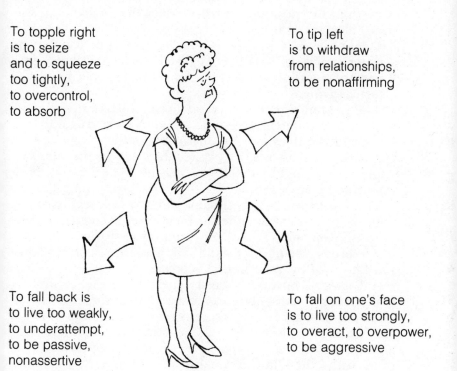

To fall back is
to live too weakly,
to underattempt,
to be passive,
nonassertive

To fall on one's face
is to live too strongly,
to overact, to overpower,
to be aggressive

To maintain a healthy
emotional equilibrium,

ASSERT AND AFFIRM

The aggressive person is pushy, a nudge, always leaning into the wind. He is off balance. His offensive stance succeeds in offending others and stimulating more aggression.

The nonassertive person shrinks back from life, withdrawing from conflict, withholding response. Defensively, he backs into life positions, retreats into safer quarters, resists the challenges of life.

Balance is the key, especially as we deal with people who are perenially off balance. To keep our own balance in a world with vertigo is no small feat. But it is necessary for effective living.

The human situation is unbalanced. Nonassertive people walk at a permanent 45° angle, bending over backwards to avoid conflict, to evade any threat. When they encounter an aggressive person who is pitched forward at the opposite angle, ready to breathe down another's neck, they have reason to be anxious.

The assertive person, maintaining a vertical balance, appears as a threat to either of the above. Recognizing he is no pushover, the aggressive person tenses for a fight. The nonassertive, seeing him stand tall, may be equally anxious, since none of his accustomed behaviors fit.

A balanced posture toward others ends the pendulum swing from nonaffirming to absorbing behavior, from nonasserting to aggressing responses. Balance exists when a state of equal concern for self and others becomes a style of life. To see others with the equal regard of appreciation; to stand with others in the equal respect of integrity; to stand for both self and others with equal rights; to work out relationships with equal responsibility—this is balance; this is equilibrium, this is strength to love and to live effectively. When the two support each other, loving tempers living. Assertive living deepens loving.

Learning to do both simultaneously is like learning to walk. We put the affirmative foot forward first; we assert by swinging our weight one step ahead. Affirmation, then assertion, step by step.

Unbalanced Living

Getting off balance is frightfully easy.

A nonassertive misstep means sacrificing one's rights in an attempt at appeasing or pacifying others. "I've no rights; I've no reason to protest anything. I won't make any waves, nice guy that I am."

An aggressive stumble means dumping your responsibility onto the other by fingering him or her as the problem. Pinning the blame on the other guy or gal lets you excuse yourself. "I can't help myself; it's all your fault. You're what's wrong with the world."

An absorbing shuffle means ditching your respect for another's integrity and seeking to lean on that person with your weight and control. "I certainly want only what's best for you. I obviously know what is best for you; I can live your life for you so much better than you could do."

A nonaffirming back-step means edging away from relationships, backing off from regarding self and other as of equal worth. "I'm worth little; I'm lucky to be allowed to eat. I doubt if you are worthful either."

Skills for being both asserting and affirming are best learned as they are seen modeled. The following section of this chapter contains exercises which can provide behavioral rehearsals for your private study and for interpersonal practice with others. Careful use of the exercises will train you in people-watching skills. As you become more aware of the kind of wholeness offered by assertive and affirmative responses, you will see them modeled by others and learn from their successes and failures. Learning by observing can be a lot less costly and painful than trial and error.

ASSERT—responsibly, rightfully.
AFFIRM—with equal respect, with equal regard.
ASSERT AND AFFIRM in wholeness.

NOT TO ASSERT IS
TO HONOR

NO RIGHTS

("I have no rights; I must
be nice, kind, self-effac-
ing, a pleaser, or else stay
quiet and safe.")

A
B
S
O
R
B
I
N
G

TO ABSORB IS
TO SHOW

NO RESPECT

("I know what is best for
you. I have only your interests at heart; I can live
your life for you so much
better than you.")

A
F
F
I

NONASSERTIVE   ASSERTING   AGGRESSIVE

M
I
N
G

NOT TO AFFIRM IS
TO OFFER

NO REGARD

("I'm worth little; I'm lucky
to be allowed to eat; I
doubt if you are worthful
either.")

N
O
N
A
F
F
I
R
M
I
N
G

TO BE AGGRESSIVE IS
TO TAKE

NO RESPONSIBILITY

("I can't help myself; you
make me angry; you drive
me up a wall. There's
nothing I can do about it.
It's all your fault.")

Experiencing Asserting and Affirming

Read the following situations; then formulate your immediate response that is both assertive and affirmative. Write it in the space provided; then compare it with the example offered. If you are tempted to read the model responses first, cover the bottom half of the page immediately before you begin to work on the situation. Writing your response before reading ours will increase your learning from the exercise. Be assertive. Be affirmative. Be both with a clear *and* linking your respect with your rights.

SITUATION ONE:
Your husband walks in the door with tiredness all over his face. The day has taken all the starch out of him. It's your night to eat out. He looks at the stove with question-mark eyebrows, then blurts, "I hope you're not planning on eating out tonight. I've had it with people, with traffic, with everything today. I'm not going anywhere."

Your response:_____

_____

_____

Modeled option:
"I can appreciate how tired you must feel. It's really been a hot and miserable day. I've got a pitcher of fresh lemonade ready. Try something cold, take a shower and relax for a half hour. Then maybe we'll both feel like having dinner somewhere cool, because I really do want to have the evening out with you."

SITUATION TWO:
Your boss is obviously irritated when he snaps off your request to leave early this afternoon to take your son for a

medical appointment. "No, arrange for someone else to get him there. We're too busy today." You're not ready to take no for an answer until he has heard how important this is to both you and the boy. If his knee is not much better when it comes out of the cast, he won't play basketball this season and you want to be there if he has to face such a disappointment.

Your response:_____

_____

_____

Modeled option:

"I want to respect and cooperate with your scheduling, *and* I want to explain how important it is for me to be at the hospital with my son this afternoon. I want to help you meet the deadline today, and I want even more to be there when the cast is removed in case it means his playing career is over, so I'd like your approval when I leave."

SITUATION THREE:

Your boss has an uncanny knack for spotting three ways any letter you type could be improved, or any report corrected to match his flawless standards. You can tolerate criticisms of mistakes, but to be faulted for choosing one of many possible right ways and then being put down as incompetent gets under your skin. After three such episodes in one forenoon, you decide to report your feelings, job or no job.

Your response:_____

_____

_____

Modeled option:

"I want to talk with you for a few minutes to clarify our working relationship since clear communications are as important to me as to you. I like working where quality is important, and I often feel that the quality of my work goes unrecognized. I appreciate suggestions for improvement, and I also get uptight when my work is compared unfavorably to another way of doing it that is only equally good. I'm sure I'll respect you much more if I feel I'm receiving equal respect from you."

Book Two.
HOW?

How people grow.
How persons change.
How behavior is learned
. . . and unlearned
. . . and relearned.

Chapter 5.
CHANGE
How Behavior Is Learned and Relearned

"One critical word, and I leave," Alex says. "If I can't just walk away from the critic, I leave mentally. I can't take criticism. I get out."

Alex has an uncanny ability to land excellent jobs, and to leave them about two years later. When the newness of his nice way of handling tensions begins to lose its effectiveness and others start reporting differences and disagreements, Alex begins composing his next letter of resignation.

"I do not criticize others. I don't like being criticized. Like my mother always said, 'If you can't say something good about another, say nothing at all.'"

Alex has a dream, a dream of a world of coworkers who do not have a critical comment behind their warm smiles. He learned this dream in his family of origin. The unruffled calm that covered his parents' denied differences was a perfect setting for learning to avoid all conflict. In fact, he overlearned this skill. His avoidance techniques are instant, automatic, virtually instinctual.

Alex wasn't born with such advanced flight reflexes. He learned to be that way. He can unlearn and relearn alternate ways of behaving in conflict situations. If he chooses, he can change, of course, but choosing the known, no matter how painful, seems more safe than risking unknown behaviors, no matter how promising. So Alex goes on choosing negative, self-defeating styles day after painful day, even when it doesn't get him the results he wants.

```
    WHY              WHY              WHY
    DO               DO               DO
     I                I                I
    DO               FEEL             ACT
   WHAT             WHAT              AS
     I                I                I
    DO               FEEL             ACT
     ?                ?                ?
```

I LEARNED IT THAT WAY!

Why such insistent choice of failure after failure?

There is one answer appropriate to most of the "why" questions you have asked about others. "Why do they act the way they do?"—they learned it that way. "Why do you have self-defeating conflicts?"—you learned it that way. "Why do you habitually irritate others or feel chronically irritated at their behaviors?"—you learned it that way!

Behavior Is Learned

Since birth, you have been learning to be you. From the scanty repertoire of behaviors that came naturally to you at birth, you have grown into the complex symphony of behaviors that you are today.

You began with a basic set of bodily responses or physiological reflexes: breathing, coughing, eye-blinking, crying. Your first cry was a natural behavior you did not need to learn. But few behaviors are innate. From a basic cluster of prewired responses, you began to branch out, adding a chuckle here and a frown there. Sounds grew into language;

movements elaborated into crawling, walking, running, and then into a whole dance of life.

Crying is the only social behavior that does not need to be learned. Some of the simplest responses, such as swallowing, are learned. (Actually it's rather complex to coordinate holding your breath and thrusting your tongue at just the right moment to force food or liquid down the correct channel. No wonder you coughed and drooled for weeks before you got it together.) And after many years of practice, you still miss cues on occasion and get food or liquids down the throat before you're ready, so that you must then clear your breathing channel with spasmodic coughing. Learning new behaviors was essential for your survival. The more appropriate the behaviors you learned, the greater your ease in survival. You learned fast because it was necessary for you to learn in order to live.

Learning Behavior Is Learning to Live with Others

Most behavior is learned in the first social setting of home, family, and playmates. First from mother, then from both parents, then siblings, peers, and finally from a whole community of people come a great stream of reinforcements that shape a child's behaviors. He or she learns skills for survival, devices for self-defense, and strategies to achieve basic recognition as a precious person.

Jim and Sue panicked when the kindergarten teacher called to complain about their five-year-old daughter. Vickie was having severe problems getting along with other children, throwing temper tantrums when she was not the center of attention, and striking other children in the face when provoked.

"I can't imagine where she ever learned it," Sue insisted. "Vickie has only Joey [a two-year-old brother] to play with at home, and he's a perfect little fellow."

When asked to describe Vickie's last temper tantrum at home, the parents insisted she was only bad at school. But gradually they admitted the hassles they were having with her daily. Finally Sue began to give an accurate description of their family behaviors.

"Last evening at the restaurant Vickie began to act up, so I told her to be quiet. She kept on making her lips move angrily at me, so I popped her in the mouth."

"Do you strike her often?"

"Sure. That's how my mom raised me. There's nothing wrong with that! I slap her when she's disrespectful."

"Do you see any connection between your violent models—hitting her frequently—and her violent behavior—striking other children?"

"Why, I'm her mother. I have the right to punish her. She's a little kid who had better do what I say, not try to do what I do."

WHICH DO YOU BELIEVE?

KIDS CAN BE CRUEL.
KIND PARENTS GET REPAID WITH PAIN.

KIDS GIVE PARENTS
WHAT THE PARENTS ASK FOR.

No matter what Sue and Jim may think, that's not how learning occurs.

Children give parents the behaviors parents ask for. Parents teach most effectively by modeling how things are to be done. And the kids learn, not what the parents think they are teaching, but what the parents are actually modeling and reinforcing in the child.

As Jim and Sue became aware of that concept, they began to see that they were training Vickie to be an assaultive child. After the shock of recognizing the obvious, they began using a whole new set of models and reinforcements for directing and limiting Vickie's behavior. In less than two weeks, rather than striking another child several times an hour, she was resorting to this destructive behavior only once every several days. After a month, hitting was almost forgotten. As the parents quit using coercive reinforcements, Vickie stopped being a coercive child.

Discovering how we learn and finding the way to relearning can free parents and children to become real people. Parents become an invitation for their children to live, and live effectively!

As you become aware of the principles of learning—how it happens and what results—you will be able to change your own behaviors. You will also be able to participate in shaping more effective behaviors in your relationships with important others.

Behaviors Are Both "Outside Acts" and "Inside States"

External behaviors, the manifest things we do, are easily observed, described, labeled. The internal responses we call "feelings" are less easy to observe since we may not really be aware of them; or we may become truly aware of what we felt in a tense situation only as we look back in hindsight (which is seldom 20/20 either).

Both internal and external responses or behaviors can be identified, monitored, and measured. There are ways of modifying both, although it is much more complex and difficult to change internal responses. The more practical route is to begin changing the external behaviors, since it is easier to act your way into a new way of feeling by changing our behaviors than it is to feel your way into a new way of acting. The first focus of growth, then, is to relearn our external behaviors. Not that the internal responses are unimportant, you understand! But the most immediate and effective steps toward change and growth occur as we alter the behaviors that affect our interpersonal relationships.

"That's just the way I am," Greg insists. "I can't change that. I've always been defensive when people criticize my work. I can't take it and I won't stand still for it." At the first sign of confrontation, Greg mobilizes his defenses. At first threat he calls out all forces. His ability to hear is sharply reduced. His anxiety shoots up to total alarm. Then Greg

YOU CAN
ACT NEW
(CHANGE IS POSSIBLE)

YOU CAN
ACT NOW
(CHANGE CAN BE IMMEDIATE)

YOU CAN CHANGE
YOU CAN GROW
(CHANGE CAN BE PERMANENT)

learns to listen until all the evidence is in, and he discovers how to hear others' comments carefully while suspending judgment. Freed from the old bind, Greg finds that his feelings are beginning to change. Anxiety drops. Defensiveness decreases.

Most internal responses (intrapersonal conflicts) are a result of external behaviors (interpersonal conflicts) that either clash or mesh with other people.

If we are in conflict with those around us—parents, children, friends, enemies—we may have any one or more of a whole spectrum of internal responses. We may feel angry, hateful, resentful, tense, confused, unloved, and so on and on.

When we are cooperating and relating smoothly with others, we may feel warm, loving, kind, happy, elated, or have some other positive response. Feeling and acting are closely related, but one discovery stands out clearly: feelings seem to be more a consequence or result of behavior than its cause. Changing behavior is a direct way of initiating change in our feeling states. With only limited control over emotions and feelings, we cannot make immediate changes at will. To change feelings, we must change behavior. Choosing a new response can elicit the parallel emotions. As behaving effectively becomes its own reward, positive feelings begin to emerge from within the self.

A case in point: Ellen is preparing to play in a violin competition. Her mother is assisting her practice by accompanying her at the piano. The phone interrupts. A friend is inviting Ellen to go swimming.

"No practice, no chance at entering the contest," mother warns.

Ellen proposes a trade. If she can play the entire piece by memory with no mistakes, she may go swimming. The contract is accepted and they begin the piece again. And again. And again.

Each time Ellen makes the same mistake her frustration increases. First she blames mother for incorrect timing; then it is the violin's fault, then a loose hair on the bow. Ellen is too rushed and too stubborn to go get her music and find her mistake. The more frustrated Ellen becomes, the more irritated mother is. Each attempt increases the tension and the anger.

Finally mother gets up, repeats the terms of their contract, and reminds Ellen she has the choice of finding her music, checking out her error, and learning to play the piece correctly, or swimming is out, by the terms of her own agreement.

Confronted with her contract, Ellen chooses to be accountable. She goes to her room, finds the music, practices for ten minutes, then returns and plays the piece without error.

Repetitive self-defeating behaviors lead to increased frustration, anger, and confusion, breaking down the desired interpersonal relationships with both mother and daughter. Because she wanted the reinforcement of swimming with her friend, Ellen took the proper steps to overcome her mistake, to inhibit the frustration, to perform adequately on the violin, to fulfill her contract and achieve her goals.

Ellen had no direct control over her emotions of anger and frustration once they were present. The only way to intervene was to change her behavior. As the behavior changed, it inhibited the distressing emotions.

Changing our behavior rewards us with positive responses

from others around us and from the need satisfactions within us. These responses inhibit the negative emotions and stimulate positive internal responses. This gives us a way to deal with our feelings rather than give in to them.

Feelings function as a barometer that indicates the pressures we are accumulating in situations of conflict or comfort. Rather than being trapped by our feelings, we can use them as a signal or a cue that something in our behavior is blocking constructive relationships with others.

I can analyze my behavior, find where the problem lies, change my behavior, and thus affect my feelings. When I use my feelings in this way I am no longer denying them, being controlled or enslaved by them, or needing to suffer through them.

I can be truly human in appreciating my feeling responses and also truly personal in responding to others constructively. Thus feelings become a rich asset rather than a painful liability.

Disturbing feelings may also be evoked by another's negative or inappropriate responses to me. I cannot change the offender's behavior but I can refuse to respond with an identical behavior that would add fuel to both of our feeling-fires.

I can change my behavior and, when I do, the flames of anger and/or aggressive behavior will die down. When the heat is off, we can behave more appropriately to each other and feel better about each other. We can see things better when we are not so emotionally charged.

Feelings are both blind and dumb, but they are part of being human. They are learned—conditioned—automatic responses. They cannot see in advance how detrimental a negative feeling may be to a person's well-being, nor do they proceed rationally, since they have no reasoning power. Logical reasoning is a thinking process, not an emotional process. Feelings come as a consequence of our behavior. As I turn to run from a growling dog, I feel fear. Later I see a similar dog, remember his tone of voice, and the old fear conditioned into me by that painful experience recurs: a new situation but the same old consequence.

Feelings are an internal consequence of behavior. To

change the feelings, I need to change my behavior. By changing my behaviors in an interpersonal conflict with my friend, or with my spouse, I can change the intrapersonal conflict inside me, that is, my feeling state.

Why All the Unadaptive Behavior?

Perhaps as high as half of the behaviors we learn in maturing are negative and unadaptive. Unfortunately, it is probably four times as difficult to unlearn unadaptive behaviors as it is to learn the adaptive behaviors the first time.

First, the unadaptive behaviors must be identified. Often it is difficult to identify our unadaptive behaviors because they occur so automatically, seem so natural, and are not recognized as unadaptive. Second, the unadaptive behaviors have to be unlearned. That is, we have to stop repeating the behaviors that seem so natural. This often results in the sense that something is missing in what we are doing. Third, we need to learn new behaviors to take the place of the old ones that we have stopped emitting. Old behavior is very tenacious, however, and has a tendency to recur long after we have forgotten about it. This recurrence of behavior is discouraging, but does not need to be so, as we will see later in the book.

A child's freedom to learn behaviors is limited by both inheritance and environment. First, the child's genetic inheritance limits the natural endowment. If he begins life with a mental defect or mental retardation, comprehension of abstract theories such as Einstein's theory of relativity will be impossible. If the child is born without hands or feet, he will experience limitations in manual skills such as typing or playing the piano, or sports skills and game playing. Although we are limited by our innate potentials, most of us possess capabilities far beyond our performance. Few people utilize more than 5 to 10 percent of their brain cells. Our capacities are so great they permit learning throughout the entire lifetime. Second, the environment may either impose limitations or excite exploration and utilization of a person's full potential. Environmental factors may stimulate learning and provide a constant stream of positive reinforcers, or they may stifle learning with negative reinforcements.

Three crucial elements in the learning process are vulnerable to breakdowns. These three—the teacher, the student, and the communications process between them—actually form the learning environment. All three are imperfect even in the best learning situations.

Imperfect Teachers

The imperfect teacher offers a mixture of behaviors, some adaptive and some unadaptive.

We begin life amid imperfect teachers—parents and family members, who are soon joined by friends, neighbors, and school instructors. Each of these offers us his own peculiar blend of functional and dysfunctional (inappropriate, nonadaptive) behaviors. A child is born with a blank behavioral slate. (Note carefully: a blank behavioral slate, not a totally blank slate. A human being is not a blank, but starts with a richly gifted slate.) The child is not free to write his own program of behaviors on his own slate because he is born helpless and is at the mercy of his parents.

The mother has the first chance to make an entry. Father and siblings add to the register. All are imperfect and write imperfectly. They misspell, mispunctuate, and misinform the child before he has opportunity or ability to edit the entries or refuse the instructions. By the time the child is able to reflect on the many instructions he has incorporated and the behaviors he has acquired, he has already learned and overlearned a high number of inappropriate and unadaptive behavioral responses.

Imperfect Students

The imperfect student distorts and confuses the teaching he or she receives. Many functional behaviors that are appropriately taught may still be misunderstood, misapplied, and mistakenly used in inappropriate ways, resulting in maladaptive behaviors. Each person understands at the level of maturity he or she has achieved. Much of what we think we are teaching a child will be above the child's ability to comprehend. Often our teaching reaches him in pieces and fragments, requiring him to integrate them and place them in order of importance. As he picks and chooses among them, what he assembles may form a crazyquilt of information that in turn results in a strange mosaic of behaviors. Since the child does not have a total view of life situations and may not be capable of considering the viewpoints of both self and others, the most appropriate fragments may result in inappropriate acts.

Determined individualism also affects the learning process. Since antiquity the human being has been aware of his limitations, but for the most part has been unable to accept them gracefully. He has often overcompensated by playing god. Thus even though our teachers may try to teach us very appropriate behaviors, we reject them: "I know better; my idea is better," etc. Often we reject the parents' (teachers') instructions for our own second-rate ideas because we can't stand having someone else look better.

Imperfect Communication

The imperfect communications system that links teacher to student magnifies and intensifies the maladaptive learnings.

Even the most highly refined and developed language system has severe limitations. At best it is only a descriptive system, a communications tool, not a communicative system. When two persons communicate, the verbal content of the message spoken and heard comprises only a small part of all that is transmitted. The tone of voice conveys the major part. And over half of the message transmitted is given by the body posture, the gestures, and the facial signs.

We cannot, in fact, fully impart what we know and experience to another. We cannot truly communicate our feelings, our understandings, or our thoughts. We can only describe them, express them, and hope that the other can receive and interpret them accurately, or in a way similar to our meanings. We cannot transfer a feeling, a value, or a viewpoint from our head to another's exactly as we understand it, feel it, or see it. There's always room for misinterpretation and misunderstanding. Each person's interpretations are filtered through that person's experience, so there is room for infinite variety and great differences.

The most powerful portion of each communication, the body language, invites even greater misunderstanding and error. Silence, for example, has many meanings. To one it indicates relaxation and meditation; to another it implies angry withdrawal; to a third it indicates empathy and listening. A blush may reveal pleasure, embarrassment, or anger. When two persons seek to communicate, the possibilities for confusion and conflict are great.

Like it or not, we live in a world of imperfect teachers offering imperfect communications to less than perfect students. If we choose, we can bemoan this conflictual mess, condemn parents and teachers alike for their inadequacy, and conclude that adequate communication is impossible, the whole interpersonal system is rotten, and the learning of functional behaviors is a hopelessly mixed process at best. Apply a little creativity to bewailing the situation, and you can probably achieve an exquisite state of misery.

There is an alternative. In spite of the many contrasting instructions inscribed on our slates in infancy and the myriad unadaptive behaviors learned in our sequence of development, we need not be victims of our circumstances. Imperfect as our interpersonal relationships and communications patterns are, they can be used in the learning of effective and appropriate behaviors. Rather than fighting our relational systems in family and community, we can capitalize on the potentials that exist. The next chapters present key principles to help you accomplish this.

Experiencing How Behavior Was Learned

Read the following conflict situation. In the space provided, note the learned behaviors and the probable learning situations you observe in the example. Then compare your hunches with the couple's own report which follows.

Situation   *Notes*

SHE: He just burns me up with his silent treatment. He walks in the door, hangs up his coat with a grunt that is supposed to pass for a greeting, then flops in a chair by the TV with the sports page across his lap, just like my dad. I ask a few questions about his day, ask if he's interested in mine, and find I'm talking to the wall. So I clam up too, and get supper on the table. He doesn't say much except "pass the bread," and then he goes outside to putter in the garage or he's back to the TV for a ball game. I get so lonely. I just can't express it. When I try, I get so negative he just shuts up all the more. He thinks I'm a real nag.

HE: I know when I'm pulling into the drive that she'll be standing there with that accusing look in her eye, and I've been scolded enough for one lifetime back at home. So I just stay out of her way. She's so full of questions, I feel like I'm on trial if I let her get going at me. I hate the word "nag." It reminds me of my mother, but that's the only word that describes her. All I want is a little peace and quiet around home after a hard day's work. I try to show that by minding my own business.

*   *   *

SHE: (After moving free from these habitual behaviors) I learned to be a nonassertive, internalizing, resenting person early in my childhood. I had an excellent model, my father. I hated my mother's nagging; I determined I'd never copy it. Now when I can't keep quiet any longer, I find I break out with prying questions, just like her, and I hate myself for it.

HE: The last thing I wanted was to live with a woman who is a "nudge." I had more than enough of that from my mother. So I courted a quiet, gentle girl who hadn't a critical bone in her. Was I ever wrong! Yes, she's quiet, but when she gets a real head of steam built up, she's just like her mother. (My wife calls her mother a real shrew.) Then I do just like my dad did when mom was an incessant nag. I shut up. I hide in the newspaper, or pretend I'm watching TV. I try to shut her out to quiet the noise. I hated it when my mom treated my dad with such silence. Here I'm doing the same thing.

For Reflection

1. Both son and daughter incorporated models from both parents.
2. Each overlearned the disliked behavior and reverts to it when the preferred behavior reaches its overload status.
3. Each is unhappy about the behavior used, yet each continues to utilize it when the cues are given by the other partner.
4. Both continue to nag and withdraw, day in, day out. The cycle of behavior never ceases. Even when apart from each other, each is anticipating the other's response, each is continuing his or her own response to the fantasized behavior. The cycle is eternal unless one of the two chooses out of the game. It takes two to play such a game. It takes one to quit.

Chapter 6.
INSIGHT
How Behavior Functions and Dysfunctions

"How could Lisa have learned to be such a bundle of conflicts?" Brian asks. "She is niney-nine percent negative, nine days a week."

Brian and Sandy are houseparents in a home for troubled girls. Lisa is their currently most-likely-to-succeed-in-starting-a-conflict prize winner.

"When I try to work with her," Brian says, "she swings back and forth from being incredibly seductive to being uncontrollably bitter, insulting, and rejecting. At seventeen, she knows how to use her sexual attractiveness to control others, and she's equally skilled at cutting men down to half their size."

"With me she acts like a little girl fishing for approval and demanding her own way at the same time," Sandy reports. "Then when she finds I set limits for her, she turns cold and cuts me up with blame and putdowns."

"Frankly, if it weren't for what I know about human behavior and how it is learned, I'd be tempted to think she's hopeless. But I won't write her off," says Brian. "Nor will I let her block out Sandy, me, or the group. She can change. I think she's beginning to want to learn some new ways of being with others. But it's almost like starting to build a person from scratch."

If you were to be of help to Lisa, would you have reason to believe change is possible? Would you expect change where she habitually conflicts with others by being alternately too sweet and clinging, or too spiteful and rejecting? What understandings of human behavior do you bring to human relationships?

This chapter will provide a basic overview of how people change. It will not only provide a more confident view of the possibilities for growth that are open to people experiencing painful conflicts; it will offer a simple clear perspective on how your own behaviors are acquired and how they can be replaced with more effective ways of relating to others.

Understanding these basic principles of human behavior will be helpful as you progress through the book. If a point seems unclear, mark it and return after reading further.

I. Behavior Is Learned

Most human behavior is learned behavior. Since it is learned, it can be unlearned. No matter how well established and how complex an inappropriate behavioral pattern is, *it can be changed*. Once we truly understand this reality, a whole new confidence about change and growth springs up in us.

II. Behavior Is Neutral

We learn negative (inappropriate or unadaptive behavior) as well as positive (appropriate or adaptive) behavior. Most behavior—in and of itself—is neutral, neither good nor bad. The behavior may or may not be appropriate to the situation in which it is used; that is, it is not adapted to the circumstance in which it occurs. It is better to refer to behavior as appropriate or inappropriate, adaptive or un-adaptive rather than right or wrong, good or bad. The behavior itself may be very useful, but it is simply out of place.

A police officer may be highly effective in restoring calm during a disturbance by standing tall and wielding powerful authority. But such a display of clout with his wife or children will spell disaster.

A salesman may be highly effective in closing important contracts by using his skill in thinking of the client's objections before they are mentioned and supplying the important data to refute them. But if he communicates with his wife or daughter in this way in his normal conversations with them, he will alienate them, or arouse their deep mistrust and suspicion.

The behaviors are neutral. But they are poorly adapted for close trusting relationships, inappropriate to intimate life. They are highly useful behaviors in certain situations, but here they are unmatched to the situation, not fitting to the context.

III. Behavior Is Habitual

Behavior changes slowly; situations change rapidly. Since much of our behavior is habitual and automatic, it may be dated, fixed, and appropriate to past situations, but curiously inappropriate to this present moment.

Habitual behaviors become firmly fixed, and require a clear effort of choice to change.

If my ability to change lags behind the pace of the changing situations, my behavior soon gets "out of date," or it goes stale. Behaviors that once got me to my goals now no longer fit. My habit of apologizing immediately when any conflict or difficulty occurs may work perfectly for pushing through crowded halls in high school when all I want is casual, smooth relationships. So I murmur, "Sorry," "Excuse me," when I tramp on someone's toes or ruffle someone's emotional feathers. But when I try building a deeper trust relationship with a college roommate, or begin serious dating, I need more than a quick apology. If I continue my habit of trying to appease and I quickly avoid any open discussion of differences, of failure, of continuing irritation with a "sorry about that," my behavior lags behind the changing needs of the evolving situations. Now I need new behaviors that confront differences and work through them to deeper understanding and respect. The wider the gap between the habitual behavior used and the new behavior needed in the new situation, the bigger the conflict will be. To decrease that interpersonal conflict, I must increase the rapidity with which I change my behavioral responses to something more effective and appropriate.

To speed up change when in new situations that require

rapid adjustment and fresh accommodation is to experience freedom to grow! Behavior is habitual, but we can make it a creative habit to adapt and adopt new behavior styles as change becomes imperative.

IV. Behavior Is Persistent

Old behavior is remarkably persistent. Often we think we have changed our behavior for good, and then find we are doing the same thing over again. This is not an exception that happens only to "weaker" people. It is the rule, true of us all. Old behavior recurs years later, given the right set of stimuli.

When the recurring behavior is a particularly noxious one, like reacting with instant violence in a family threat situation, it may seem especially discouraging to have it recur in a moment of high anxiety. There is no need to panic when an old negative behavior recurs. Making a mistake can be a useful experience. The unexpected return of an old behavior can show in contrast how much we have grown. It can confirm our intention to respond in more effective ways. At times it may stimulate us to search for totally new ways of behaving. If we have only one or two behaviors to use when threatened by others, any stimulation to invent, or learn additional ways of responding is a stimulation to growth. So when an old unwelcome behavior reappears, we can use it as an incentive to creative growth—a victory, not a defeat.

Eventually, we will desensitize ourselves to many of the stimuli that cause us to summon old unwanted behaviors out of storage and allow them to block our new ways of relating. Rarely is old behavior totally eliminated, though it will occur less and less frequently. Thus a recurrence need not be expected, but it can be accepted and managed effectively when it does emerge from our personal museum of learned ways of behaving.

V. Behavior Is Operant

How we operate as persons affects how others operate with us. What we give, we get. As we act, we invite and elicit responses from others. Any behavior affects the behavior that follows, which in turn affects the next in a continuous chain of operations. Thus behavior is said to be "operant." A husband who withdraws into silence behind a newspaper or TV for an evening may trigger a "nagging" response from his wife. Her sharp criticisms of his silent treatment will likely increase his clamming up to spite her. The one person's behavior operates (affects) the behavior of the other. Her nagging reinforces his withdrawing. His flight stimulates her fight!

Most persons get a lot of inappropriate responses from others because they behave inappropriately. Learning to behave in a positive way will invite and often insure positive responses from others. This can help shape other people's behavior to become more healthful, pleasurable, effective, and satisfying. Unfortunately, most of us have learned so much negative behavior that we more frequently shape ineffective and unsatisfying responses in others than vice versa. Such a self-defeating state of affairs snowballs because behavior is operant.

In addition—and here lies the crucial secret—behavior is affected by its consequence, modified by the effects it has on others, and thus shaped by its results. If the behavior achieves its desired results, it will be repeated. Persons who eat heavily whenever anxious, threatened, or bored will find the consequences—comfort for anxiety, distraction from the threat, active interest in food to escape boredom—a regular reinforcer. When they want comfort, or distraction, or excitement, they eat. If there are painful consequences, we will be more likely to try to discover better ways to reach the goal, more appropriate ways to get what we need and want, or more satisfying ways to relate to others.

Thus, when we say behavior is operant, we mean not only that it affects what follows, but also that it is affected by what follows. It is an operation that produces consequences, and those desired consequences reproduce the same operation in similar circumstances. This cycle is the normal operation of the human person. Fortunately, it can be interrupted, altered, reshaped.

VI. *Behavior Is Not the Behave-er*

Behavior and the behave-er are not one and the same. I am not my behavior. You are not your behavior. My behavior is mine but it is not me. I am more than my behavior, since in the next moment I am free to choose a new way of responding, a different way of behaving. If you dislike my actions or object to my behavior, report your objections and feelings. But do not attack me, label me, or judge me as being only that one way of responding.

A person's behavior is an expression of the person's experience, but it is not the person nor is it his or her whole experience. A behavior is only a part of the whole, not the whole person. A lie told does not make a person a liar (a lie is an isolated act, a liar is a person who possesses a permanent or habitual style of relating). An act of stealing does not make a person a thief. (To steal is an inappropriate be- havior, it is not an indication of a continuing practice of lifestyle.) Often labels are attached immediately to people when they engage in inappropriate behavior.

Behavior must be seen as separate and distinct from the person. Otherwise, any criticism becomes an attack on the person and stimulates a response of self-defense. A bit of insulating distance will be helpful in making a clear differen- tiation between both one's own and the other's behavior. When two wires connected to the poles of a charged battery are held too close, sparks will jump the gap, generate heat, and radiate energy. Separate the wires a safe distance, and the poles can conserve their energy without the fireworks. When two persons stand at opposite poles, the emotional electrodes are separated by an insulating distance that will diffuse the conflicting emotions and greatly diminish the charged relationships. Each can then deal with the other's behavior while respecting his person and affirming his worth. Thus the differences can be resolved with fewer impulsive explosions and more helpful behavioral changes.

VII. *Behavior Is Chosen*

I choose how I want to behave. You choose how you want to behave. We are in control of our own behavior. No one else can make us think, feel, act as we do. My behavior represents my ability to respond. Your behavior indicates your response-ability.

Most persons tend to either take too much responsibility, or too little responsibility, or both at the same time. To take too little is to attempt to blame others for one's own behavior. This is frequently expressed in the charges "You make me angry," "You made me do what I did," "You're responsible for my pain, frustration, failure, etc., etc." Such demands that another take responsibility for my behavior are inappropriate and ineffective as well as impossible. To take too much responsibility is to seek to control and manage other persons' behavior. This intensifies frustration, instigates guilt and anger, and blocks constructive relating. We are not responsible for each other's behavior. Nor are we responsible *to* each other in behaving according to others' demands. We are most effective as we seek to be responsible *with* each other in gentle affirmation and genuine assertiveness.

VIII. *Behavior Is Distorted*

In our human society, fear, threat, anxiety, injustice, violence, and coercion are common. Rather than rewarding creativity and cooperation, society takes these for granted and centers its attention largely on controlling its ills. Our behavior is then distorted by negative feedback of punishment, insistence on conformity, and worship of the status quo, all of which stifle our natural creativity, our growth and unfolding as persons. At work, a supervisor may feel threatened by a suggestion from an employee and respond negatively even though the idea is outstanding. At home, a child may move toward greater self-respect and freedom, but in a way differing from the family's usual patterns. As the parent restricts the choices and reprimands the child, growth is stunted.

The distortions of our imperfect human social system— imperfect teachers, imperfect students, imperfect communication processes—all contribute to our learning much unadaptive behavior which we continually need to recycle, relearn, or replace with more adaptive positive behavior.

Most of us have learned so much negative behavior that it serves as the major component of our behavioral repertoire. The stronger, more dominant behavior—the one we have learned best and use most—tends to overpower and inhibit the weaker behavior. If I have overlearned unadaptive behaviors (how to manipulate, how to coerce, how to cling possessively, how to sponge off of others dependently), then these will tend to inhibit the positive forms of these same responses (how to relate equally, how to negotiate respectfully, how to love, how to practice self-care).

So behavior is distorted toward the unadaptive side by many of the forces of society, community, and family. But this too can be unlearned, and relearned in adaptive ways.

IX. Behavior Can Transcend Conditions

Although behavior is conditioned by past learning experiences and present living situations, courageous behaviors can be willed, firmly chosen, and resolutely held even in the face of almost overwhelming social criticism or rejection.

When a person has come to prize values as ultimately worthful, he or she may commit his or her behaviors in decisive choice and accept the consequences, be they negative or positive reinforcers. When such choices are viewed as unadaptive by the society, the person may suffer extreme rejection, coercion, and even martyrdom. Erratic behaviors or disordered choices may require that others take careful responsibility for the person as long as he or she remains emotionally disturbed or mentally confused, and unaware of his or her behavior and its effect on others. The responsibility to protect both the person and the community is awesome, and those who assume it must be ordered by moral values which respect the equal worth of persons and provide equal opportunity both for care and for justice.

At the opposite extreme are those whose moral values transcend the culture's practices and stimulate them to stand against the culture in criticism and confrontation of its practices. Aleksander Solzhenitsyn, a man of such universal principle, models the integrity possible to the person who affirms human values and willingly accepts the consequences of such a choice. All the potency of the Soviet State was frustrated by the courage of his unconditional choice. Such courage has often been annihilated by violence, yet stands invincible in the memories of humankind.

X. Behavior Is Process

To behave is to be in process, to be responding, relating to others, repeating old learnings or learning new behavior.

A behavior style can be a defensive process that relies totally on past learnings and braces itself against the threat of change. On the other hand, one can choose a behavior process that is constantly unlearning unadaptive options, learning more appropriate alternatives, and increasing the richness of relationships. Such a behavior style is reflective, examining life to gain as much information about self and others as possible. It is objective, seeking to base conclusions on as much clear data as available rather than on assumptions or prejudices. It is creative, open to new truth and willing to change when new evidence or new experience invalidates the old.

What are the essentials of this process? In this chapter we have noted that behavior is learned and can be relearned; it is neutral and must be matched appropriately to various situations; it is habitual and changes slowly; it is persistent and recurs when triggered by the paired stimuli; it is operant and both affects what follows and is affected by what follows in consequence. We have learned that a person's behavior is not the person, but behavior is chosen by the person; behavior is often distorted by the negatives of our society, yet it can transcend conditions, even the worst of situations.

If some of this summary seems unclear, review, rethink, react . . . and relearn.

Reviewing Principles of Behavior

Each of the following ten examples illustrates one of the ten principles of behavior outlined in this chapter. Using Example 1 as a model, fill in the remaining blanks with the appropriate concepts.

1. I told myself over and over, I'll never talk to my kids in the critical tone of voice my mother used. But when they get on my nerves, I do it. Even though I resented it, I <u>learned</u> her behavior.

2. I'm confused. I can outthink a customer and outsmart his objections without irritating him at all. But when I read my wife's mind and outmaneuver her in an argument she gets furious. I get promoted for doing it at the office, I get demoted at home. The behavior must be _____; it's my inappropriate use that creates the problem.

3. I could always get off the hook with my dad by eating humble pie, by groveling a little. He'd soon quit criticizing and scolding. Now whenever I get into a bind with others, I grovel a little. It seldom works but I do it in any threat situation. It's virtually automatic. I feel the threat, I respond _____.

4. I can't believe it. I've made all kinds of contracts with my wife; I've rehearsed new responses with a counselor, and I plan to respond in new ways. But every now and then I still slip back into my old way of clamming up and swallowing stress for a couple days and then I blow up with temper and come out with some stale grievance from long ago. Old behavior is incredibly _____.

5. I come home tired of being with people all day; I just want a moment's silence. My wife has been bored with her work and is eager to talk. I pick up the paper and settle behind it in a chair. She sits on the arm and begins talking. I grow more silent. She talks more intensely. I get irritated. She becomes frustrated and gives up. I now have the silence I want, but I'm tense with the consequences. I resolve not to let this happen again. The next evening I try to be even more effectively quiet. My wife gets the message and lets me unwind alone, but the atmosphere is even more tense. My behavior produces the wanted consequences, but the side effects are frustration and more frustration. It's like a cyclical trap, the way we operate with each other. Our behavior is _____.

6. "I am a born loser," I said, as I looked at the mangled fender on my boss's car. I borrowed it for a quick errand. I backed into a fire hydrant. "I'm a jinx!" (So I did make a mistake. Is that reason enough to identify me the _____ by my _____?)

7. I get really fed up with your nudging and I finally say, "You make me so angry, you drive me up a wall with your insensitive criticism. You are always cutting me down, you crank." (I am refusing to admit that my behavior is _____ _____.)

8. I sometimes reflect on how smooth relationships could be if each of us responded appropriately to another, but behavior is always mixed. Responses are invariably misunderstood to some extent. And somehow quotations get twisted, intentions become confused, and trust is betrayed. It seems that even the best of relationships elicit behavior that is _____.

9. I've every reason to resent the guy. He's circulated rumors about me that have no basis in reality. He reported my coming late to the supervisor without checking that I had requested permission the day before. He's out to get me. I could resent him, but I recognize it's his problem. I refuse to have my reactions controlled by his actions. My behavior can

_____ the conditions. I can choose to _____ the circumstances.

10. I obviously haven't arrived. But I'm becoming what I want to be. I guess the best way to say it is that I'm in

_____.

(Check back through the chapter to compare your descriptive word choice with the principles of behavior outlined. If you got most of ten, reward yourself!)

Experiencing How Inappropriate Behavior Is Learned

Behavior is learned in a setting that is purposeful, functional, reward-winning. But that setting may not come again. Or it may be repeated only in part so that the old learned response is triggered automatically but fits only fragmentarily. There is nothing wrong with the old behavior; it just doesn't match the situation. In the following exercise, study the two examples that are given. Then use the lefthand column to describe behaviors you frequently use that in hindsight you find are less than appropriate. In the middle column, indicate the situation in which you used the behavior; then, in the righthand column, list situations where the behavior may have optimum use and impact.

Behavior	Inappropriate Situation	Appropriate Situation
"Nice-nice" placating and appeasing behavior designed to induce another to excuse my failure.	Used to avoid any honest confrontation with my wife, or to silence any frank criticism from colleagues.	Useful for a small powerless child before an angry tyrannical parent, or for an anxious person before a belligerent drunk.
Guessing another's motives, reading the other's intentions. Judging another's reasons.	Seeking to blame another for unacceptable motives which I "know" are true.	Seeking to empathize with another's concerns and understand from their point of view.

Experiencing Respect for Behavior and Behave-er

The behavior is not the behave-er. I am not my behavior—my behavior is an expression of my response-
abilities at the moment. You are not your behavior—your
behavior simply expresses your ability to respond at this
moment. To experience this crucial difference work
through the following exercises reflecting on yourself; then
rehearse giving the same freedom and dignity to others.

My View of My Behavior	*My View of Me, the Behave-er*
I am intensely angry, I am thinking violent thoughts, I would like to tell the other to drop dead, I have an impulse to wish he or she were annihilated!	I am thinking murderous thoughts. Am I a murderer? No . . . I am the thinker, I am not the thought. I am free to refuse it, to rise above it, to respond in angry concern, not angry coercion.
I am embarrassed. I just lost my temper and blurted out a very cutting and belittling remark to my wife. What a dirty way to fight! I have found a painful spot in her and trampled on it.	I am an insensitive crank. A cold, cutting, self-centered egotist? No . . . I am the speaker, not the spoken word. In the next moment I can apologize, I can change my response, I can go beyond it.
I feel defeated. I just blew it. I had the perfect chance to get the promotion and I got defensive in the interview and got my foot in my mouth. I'm a born loser.	I am an inadequate and inferior person. No . . . I am the actor, not the actions. I acted as if I were much less adequate than I know myself to be. I can learn from the experience.

Exercising Your Ability to Differentiate

Complete the following:

Your View of Conflictual Behavior	*Your Stance as Behave-er*
1. I am troubled when I've been thinking	1. I am the thinker, not the thought, so
2. I am angry that I acted inappropriately by	2. I am the actor, not the action, so
3. I feel guilty that I failed to	3. I am the fail-er, not the failure, so
4. I am frustrated that my performance at the piano (or other) was so miserable	4. I am the performer, not the performance, so

5. I am so resentful of him
for

_____

_____

5. I am the resenter, not
the resentment, so

_____

_____

6. I have messed up so often
I am a lousy person

_____

_____

6. I am not my past; I am
who I am now, so

_____

_____

Chapter 7.

SECRETS

How Behavior Is
Conditioned and Reconditioned

The Reverend Carl James is the king of the nice guys. It is rumored that he was once seen without his perma-smile, but no one knows who made the sighting.

The more tense the situation, the nicer, more ingratiating he becomes.

"I guess I'm a chronic pleaser," Carl admits warmly as we talk about the conflicts he is having with his church. "I've always wanted to keep people unruffled, to not make waves, to have everybody happy. But it's more than I can do. In fact, it seems that the more I try to get close to people, the less they trust me."

(I'm aware that the longer he talks, the more guarded I feel. His sweetness seems seductive, as if he's slipping something past me.)

A Simple Unit of Behavior

Obviously Carl has a problem relating effectively to people in any threatening situation. (That is, this is obvious to anyone but Carl. He just smiles harder, and comes on softer.) His one response to the stimulus of threat is smiling sweetness and copious agreement. The consequences of this habitual choice are increased mistrust and distance between himself and others. This is the exact opposite of what he wants.

98

The stimulus (S) of threat elicits the response (R) of appeasing which produces the consequences (C) of false closeness and suspicion. These three elements, stimulus-response-consequences, make up the smallest basic unit of behavior. At times the SRC sequence is called the ABC of behavior, "A" being the antecedent or activating event evoking the behavior "B" which results in consequence "C." These three elements form the fundamental unit of human behavior. Even the most complex pattern of behavior can be broken down into its essential parts, each of which possesses its own stimulus, response, and consequences.

"How and when did you learn to be a pleaser?" I ask Carl. He reviews the many experiences of youth and childhood with a fixed smile. "I think it was early, very early. My parents were firm, even a bit harsh. They used to really punish me when I was bad. My dad didn't mind taking a strap to us kids. And I got my share. I guess I learned to stay on his good side. From age three or four on, I've been a real smiler."

The threat of whipping was a powerful stimulus for little Carl. His response was to smile, please, and appease the feared authority. The consequence was a nice phoniness which served him well by insuring a distance from the danger while also holding him at an effective distance from trusting relationships. Carl has learned this sequence brilliantly. In any situation of real or imagined threat, he oozes sweetness. This multiplies mistrust and increases distancing until any closeness is seen as threat. His smile is standard equipment. "How can anyone be uncomfortable with me when I'm always warm and understanding?" he protests. Oblivious to the obvious, he continues the vain attempt at appeasing.

Complex Units of Behavior

Carl James is not only a "pleaser." This is only one of the behaviors he uses. It is his most common response to threat. And it's his least effective. It creates more suspicion than trust. Trust is what he both wants and needs. Carl can be open and at times is willing to risk sharing deeply. Then people trust him more. He is a complex man with many skills, many sides, many different behaviors.

BEHAVIOR MAKES SENSE

A = **Activating Event**
(Stimulus)

B = **Behavior**
(Response)

C = **Consequences**
(Either positive or negative results, which become a new stimulus for the next response)

Human beings are highly complex. One sequence of behavior, such as smiling sweetly when on the spot, can be easily broken down to its constituent parts. The stimulus, the response, and the consequence can be clearly seen. But often things move so rapidly that a person's behavior seems to make no sense to him or to anyone watching. Both the actor and the observer may be confused. When so many conflicting responses are happening so quickly between persons, they may despair of understanding themselves or interrupting the self-defeating SRC sequence.

Untangling the knots in our relationships can be more exciting than reading a whodunit. Here the key questions are "What did I do?" and "How did I do it?" When I can see what I did and how I did it, the SRC sequence in my actions will become clear. Often a number of these sequences overlap or interact so that a whole tangle of SRC units are woven together and ensnarling each other. If I can find which is the basic SRC unit, an immediate change at the basic level can be planned which will then alter the whole sequence of reactions.

Next Sunday Ima Krank will stop Carl James to say, "You preached too long, you didn't say anything, and you didn't look at me once." The threat of her criticism may trigger his very nicest smile and his vain attempt to appease her anger with graceful groveling. Or he may respond firmly and authentically, "Ms. Krank, I think the sermon was one of my best." His new assertiveness will bring new responses from her.

ASK YOURSELF . . .

1. What hit me?
(Stimulus)

2. What did I do?
(Response)

3. What did it get me?
(Consequences)

Newton's law, "For every action there is an equal and opposite reaction," is as true in human behavior as it is in physics, although it is less easily traced. The SRC formula, in essence, affirms the same inevitability. For every response there is a stimulus; for every response there is a consequence. Rarely, if ever, does a behavior occur which was not stimulated by some identifiable event. Singling out that event is made easier by knowing that the same stimulus and response and event are frequently and consistently paired. Behavior does not occur out of the blue. Something has always preceded and affected it; something always results as a consequence. It may be difficult to identify the stimulus when it is quite distant from the behavior. Today's response may be to yesterday's stimulus.

Delayed Responses

For example, Fred has a friend, an alcoholic named Gus, who has been trying to break his drinking habit and has abstained for three months. Seeing the free bar at the union meeting, Fred decides to intervene if he spots Gus going for a drink. Gus moves towards the bar, so Fred hurries to offer him a cup of coffee. Before he can reach him, Gus turns his back to the bar.

At work the next week, Fred compliments Gus for resisting the urge to drink.

In congratulating Gus, Fred is responding to a stimulus that occurred several days earlier. Gus is refusing a present stimulus in favor of one he received at the Alcoholics Anonymous meeting a week before. At times the stimulus may have occurred weeks, months, or even years before the response occurs. That is, behavior is a response to a stimulus which has in all likelihood been long forgotten. This distance between stimulus and response frequently makes it difficult for us to understand the reason we behave the way we do. "It doesn't make sense," we may say; "there wasn't any reason for me to behave that way." Applying the SRC formula to our experiences may help us track down the stimulus that kicked off a behavior even though the particular stimulus was presented a long time ago. As we identify the stimuli, and recognize the connection, behavior will be less mystical, more understandable, and the possibility of change more feasible.

Conditioned Responses

A year ago, before going on the wagon, Gus would have hit the bar instantly. At that time his drinking behavior was so habitual and ingrained, he scarcely gave it a thought. The stimulus of clinking ice in glasses brought immediate response of dry-mouth. The sight of the free bar then would have drawn him into downing one drink after another without any evaluative thought. Much of Gus's behavior occurred without his being aware of it. Gus was highly conditioned in his responses.

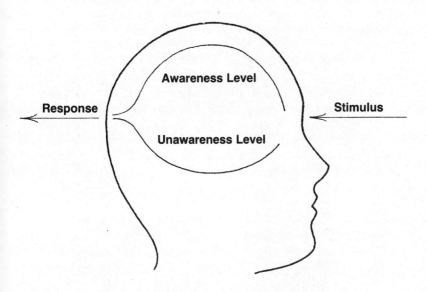

THE CONDITIONED RESPONSE IN ADVERTISING

1. I see commercials for a shaving cream that are subtly erotic and arouse unaware responses of excitement with the product.
2. I am choosing between shaving products at the store, and I receive the same erotic signals from the package; an unaware excitement focuses my attention on the brand.
3. I buy it in response to the excitement on the unawareness level.

When we first learn a behavior, we frequently do so at the aware or conscious level. As we learn, we think about the behavior and practice it as we do it. Learning also occurs below the level of awareness. This unaware level of learning is frequently used by skilled persuaders. Advertising may be designed to trigger a response on the unawareness level.

In the above diagram the S→R→C line is divided into two levels—awareness and unawareness. When a new behavior is well learned, we no longer think about it. It becomes a conditioned response, a habit, a reflex action.

When the stimulus is presented, the response is automatic. The learned behavior is performed without aware thought.

Pictorially speaking, we may place the conditioned response below the level of the eyebrows. We see and react without thinking about it, whereas the learned response occurs at the level of awareness, i.e., above the level of the eyebrows. The cortex of the brain, the level in which cognitive processes are located, lies essentially above the level of the eyebrows. (Neurologically, this is only partially accurate; practically, this distinction helps us conceptualize the levels of awareness or unawareness, of habitual or volitional responses, of conditioned or conscious behaviors.)

Automatic Responses

Joan grew up as the second girl in a family of three. Both her older and younger sisters conformed easily to their parents' wishes. Joan resisted. Throughout her teenage years, her father carried on a running warfare with her through his constant criticism, moralizing, and demands. To cope with his continuous pressure, Joan withdrew to a safe detachment, permitting herself few feelings and interacting with him only on the level of ideas and arguments. This conscious aware choice has now become an unaware, habitual response to closeness with any adult male.

Now Joan is married to a man whose rich feelings and open emotional experience attracted her greatly. But when they move close, she turns into a computer. Arguments, theories, ideas are all used to maintain distance. The closeness she endorses so brilliantly seems impossible for her to tolerate emotionally.

Joan is cold and distant at the very moments she "thinks" that she wants to be close. When she wants to be intimate, she finds her mind is going at top speed. When she wants to respond sexually, she finds she has lost touch with her body and senses. She has fled into her computer room.

Closeness to a man means criticism and demands to Joan. Her unaware reflexive response to this stimulus is to close up and become cerebral. This is an excellent skill for dealing with her IRS auditor, or for facing an oral exam when completing her master's degree. But now her behavior lags behind the changing situation. The new situation—marriage and intimacy—calls for different behavior. The behavioral gap between her habitual response and the response she needs in order to live effectively is creating intense conflict within her and within her marriage. Her reflexive, unaware behavior must be made conscious and aware if change is to occur.

If the proverbial doctor with his rubber hammer is testing your knee reflex, you kick in an automatic "reflexive" response. There is no conscious thought. You kick in reaction to the stimulus presented to the tendon. The sharp blow below the knee stretches the receptors in the muscle, sending a signal to the spinal cord, not to the brain, and the signal is instantly sent back to the muscles causing the knee to jerk. Since the circuit does not go to the brain, we call it a reflex. In a parallel way, conditioned responses form a reflex type of action at the unaware level without passing the signal on to the aware level of the brain. We see something, feel something, or hear something, and respond automatically.

When you touch a hot stove, your hand is quickly withdrawn without conscious choice. When you hear rejection in another's tone of voice, defensive feelings or angry signals occur automatically without aware decision. An angry response can be learned so well that it becomes habitual and the immediate response to the person who criticizes us is to strike back.

Tracking Down Stimuli

Mark, a pharmacist in his forties, reports that he is frequently overcome by intense temper episodes, especially when he sees a larger boy teasing, harassing, or fighting with a smaller boy. He has become so enraged when seeing mistreatment of children in films or on TV that he is violently angry for hours. He is totally baffled by his outbursts.

When reflecting on his childhood, Mark refers several times to his older brothers and their rough handling of him and his younger brother. "They used to grab me by the ankles and hold me back when I wanted to get away from them," he recalls. Suddenly, his response makes sense. As he views this memory according to the SRC formula, he can see how the unaware response to an old stimulus produces inner rage. On the unaware level, he has now generalized the stimulus to include all mistreatment of all kids and all powerless persons in any coercive situation. The unaware response reduces him to an impotent rage.

As Mark recognizes the SRC sequence in his flashes of temper, his emotional response is brought from unawareness to the level of awareness, and he becomes free to identify what is appropriate to the present situation and what is inappropriate and useless. Now he is able to make a clear choice of a useful response—in this case, firm assertiveness in interrupting an injustice to a child.

Recycling Old Patterns

Old behaviors can be recycled. The concern for justice that Mark feels so deeply is a beautiful and valuable part of the man. To lose it would be sad. But the way Mark is expressing it in violent and abusive anger is defeating to himself and to his goals. He needs to recycle an old behavior pattern to bring it up to date from a response suited to a four-year-old to a behavior useful to a man of forty.

Recycling a behavior pattern brings it up from the level of unawareness, examining it in aware thought processes, and learning new behavior. Eventually the new way is learned so well that it occurs without conscious thought as a habitual "reconditioned" response.

By recycling behavior we can decrease the gap between our response and the requirements of the situation around us. This decreases conflict and leads to more effective and comfortable living. When we feel conflict inside—tension, anxiety, guilt, anger—it is a very useful signal that change and growth are needed. Old behaviors are slowing our growth as persons. Recycle! Catch up! Conflict is a signal that it may be time for recycling or relearning.

Recycling can be initiated by beginning at any one of the following three points.

I. Removing Old Stimuli

Once we've identified an old unadaptive behavior, we can begin plotting an appropriate way to go about changing. The first way is to remove the stimulus, if this is possible or practical. If we cannot get rid of it, we can work to become desensitized to the stimulus. When a hot stove is burning you, you remove your hand. The painful stimulus can be instantly removed. If an obnoxious neighbor is the negative stimulus and the mere presence of the person in your backyard sets off a great amount of frustration, tension and anger, the removal of the stimulus is not an appropriate option (although board fences are frequently built). A better step is to desensitize yourself, either by seeing a therapist or working through with an insightful friend so that you can relax, cancel your demands that the neighbor live as you prescribe, lower your anxiety, and learn more appropriate behaviors for decreasing conflict.

II. Replacing Old Behaviors

The second way we can change behavior is to make a rational, volitional decision that the behavior we are performing is not in our best interests. Major changes require clear, aware choice-making. When we view our behavior with the predetermined conclusion that it can't be changed, we make feeble efforts to alter it (we fulfill our own prophecy).

We can choose to change behavior because of two unique skills: the ability to recall past experience and the capability to visualize. We can choose freely because we can predict positive results before ever having received any. Trust in similar learned experiences, although they are not identical, reinforces the choice. Because of the ability to delay gratification, we can make changes even though they are not immediately reinforced. Future consequences of current behavior can be anticipated and enjoyed in fantasy before they become reality.

III. Restructuring the Consequences

The third way to change behavior is to restructure the consequences. If the rewards are changed, the behavior can be changed.

Each behavior has its own payoff. Behaviors are repeated or not because of some meaningful consequence to each response. If the payoff is positive, we will continue to repeat the same behavior. If the payoff is negative or aversive, then we are more likely to change our behavior to escape the negative consequences. Thus, one can change his behavior by restructuring the consequences so there is a new and positive payoff to the behavior he sees is in his best interest.

For example, if a child has homework to do but no interest in doing it, the reward offered can change the study behavior immediately. If he has a favorite television program to watch later in the evening, mother can restructure the consequences so that it pays off for him to finish his studying: he can earn the privilege of watching television after he has done his homework. This is often called "grandma's rule," or "work after play."

The restructuring of consequences has been in use for a long time and is a classic principle of human behavior. Most persons do this continuously and automatically to motivate themselves to do unpleasant jobs. They do the disliked job first, then reward themselves with a pleasant experience.

Not only can we change by restructuring consequences for ourselves, we can help others change their behavior by helping them get the desired payoff. We can also invite them to help us grow and change. We can contract to help each other mature, relate more effectively, and build community.

Experiencing Behavioral Sequences

Learning to identify the elements of your behavior sequences can help clarify the habitual responses you make to the many stimuli you receive. As you become able to break down the events of your experiences into the basic units of behavior you can initiate change in a planned and systematic way.

SRC (stimulus-response-consequence) sequences spiral and interconnect. The consequence becomes the stimulus for the next response. A negative response will most frequently produce a negative consequence, which functions as a new negative stimulus and triggers a further negative response, and so on and so forth. This negative snowball effect can add insult to injury to injustice.

When reversed, this snowballing of stimulus-response-consequence-to-new stimulus-etc. can be an upward spiral of positive responses that free the relationship. Then each interchange builds on the previous one: each interaction surpasses the one before.

To recognize when a spiral is going downhill and to reverse the process by inverting the cycle of responses is to make behavioral insights work for you.

1. Examine the following sequence of behaviors.

2. Reflect on a recent conflict of your own and fill in three sequences of your own responses.

3. Consider how negative sequences could be reversed.

4. Rehearse ways to respond positively and more powerfully.

5. Reread the model sequence and your charted behaviors.

6. Identify nonassertive, assertive, and aggressive responses.

7. Label nonaffirmative, affirmative, or absorbing attitudes.

8. Make notes for new assertive and affirmative responses you want to use in the future.

Stimulus	Response	Consequence
1. The car broke down, requiring major repairs which may not be worth the investment.	2. I went to the dealer to investigate trading cars. I looked at the car I'd liked to have, then asked for an appraisal of mine.	3. The salesman wanted a deposit on the new car before making an estimate on the value of the old car.
4. His demands for an instant sale and a deposit on the line triggered intense frustration in me.	5. I told him what a second-rate dealership they were operating and what a questionable sales game they were playing and assured him he'd not get any business from me.	6. I walked out of the place angry at the salesman and with him angry at me.
7. I went to another dealer, still angry about the previous salesman's strategy.	8. I snapped at the salesman as soon as he mentioned he would need someone else to give an estimate on my old car.	9. He told me I could wait for the manager, that he didn't enjoy making estimates for someone as upset as me. I walked out of the second shop.

Stimulus	*Response*	*Consequence*
10. I was doubly frustrated, aware that I was putting my anger for the first salesman onto the second one.	11. I went back into the store and apologized to the salesman, telling him my irritability was triggered by the previous salesman.	12. We both laughed as our tenseness dissipated. We began to look at his cars, and he ordered an estimate on my old one.

S ———————→ R ———————→ C

Stimulus ———→ *Behavior* ———→*Consequence*

1.

      2.

          3.

4.

      5.

          6.

7.

      8.

          9.

Chapter 8.
REWARDS
How Change Is
Reinforced or Enforced

"You touch that TV set one more time and I'll beat your bottom in with a shoe," the father yells at his three-year-old, who insists on turning the color adjustment dial. A moment later the little fellow is back at it again. More threats are yelled, and he scampers off for a few minutes. The ninth time the child is at the set, the father picks him up by the arm and begins to pound at him with an old slipper. "No-good kid," he mutters, "I'll teach you to obey me when I tell you to let that TV alone."

The father is teaching the little fellow, and teaching well. But not what he thinks he's teaching. Children give parents what the parents ask for. And this father is asking for the little fellow to grow up defiantly, getting attention by testing out his father's empty threats until his temper is aroused, then accepting the whipping stoically, knowing well that the father will feel guilty about his violence afterward and for a period the boy can do anything he wants, ask for anything he wishes, get away with anything he tries.

Teaching and learning happen by rewards. The payoff is what keeps the behavior going. If we get the kind of payoff we want, we are more likely to repeat those behaviors. If we do not get the kind of payoff desired, we are less likely to do those behaviors.

The payoff reinforces behavior. A reinforcer or reinforcement is anything that strengthens something. When a builder reinforces concrete he puts in structural steel to strengthen the wall. If he builds with wood, he reinforces the framing with cross braces. When a platoon is reinforced, more recruits are added. To change, shape, or reshape behavior, old reinforcements are taken away and new reinforcers are added to initiate the new behavior. When the payoff or consequences are reinforcing, the behavior is likely to occur more frequently. When the consequences are nonreinforcing or there is no payoff, they weaken the behavior, decrease it, and finally extinguish it. Behavior is extinguished (or drops out) when it is not reinforced. When we get nothing out of it, we quit doing it. Aversive, unpleasant consequences usually result in extinguishing or weakening a behavior. When it hurts more than helps, we quit trying it.

The person who gives the most reinforcement receives the most reinforcement. This is the behavioral golden rule. "Treat others as you want them to treat you." Said another way, "You get what you give." Unfortunately, most of us apply the golden rule in reverse. We usually wait until someone else is nice to us, that is, gives us positive reinforcement, before we positively reinforce him or her. When we unscramble the golden rule and apply it, then we give first and get the like in return.

Each of us seems to have an internal bookkeeping system of accounting for the love shown us or the pain that we receive. In the long run the behavioral books have a way of evening out. Old scores are settled either on the level of awareness or the level of unawareness. We remember the stimuli received from the other persons. Eventually, we get our payback. Others remember, aware or unaware, to pay out their accounts to us. If we have paid out in positive reinforcement, we will be more likely to receive positive behavior back. If we have paid out in negative reinforcement, we will get negative behavior back. People have an uncanny ability to remember the negative things someone has done to them. We may not get our negative payback for years but eventually the back pay arrives.

In summary, we can change our behavior or shape the behavior of other people by arranging the proper reinforcers. We can also extinguish unwanted behavior by no longer reinforcing it. By using these two processes in combination, we can make gradual but major changes in our own as well as in the behavior of those with whom we relate. In the next section we will examine the eight major types of reinforcers.

I. Positive and Negative Reinforcement

If you want to change behavior, you can reinforce either positively or negatively. Both are effective. However, positive reinforcement is effective in both changing and maintaining behavior. Negative reinforcement changes the response, but does not maintain change. The minute the negative reinforcement is withdrawn, the unwanted behavior recurs. In addition, negative reinforcement saturates or satiates. After a while people get saturated and stop responding to negative reinforcement.

A parent who repeatedly spanks a child to get him or her to do the things he wants finds that eventually the child no longer responds. In spite of repeated spanking, he or she keeps on emitting the unacceptable behavior.

Positive reinforcement rewards the desired behavior rather than penalizing the undesired response. Most occupations give salary checks for cooperative and productive employee behavior. You do the job and you get paid in reward. Few jobs use negative reinforcement by giving the salary in advance and then charging the employee for any error or absenteeism. This may be an effective way to change a behavior, but it does not maintain the change.

When a child is doing poorly in school, parents often use negative reinforcement. They may take away television viewing or cut the child's allowance or recreational privileges in order to get him to do his studying. This will force immediate change, but it will be short-lived. Reinforce positively whenever possible. If lack of sufficient positive reinforcements forces occasional use of negative reinforcement, it is important to give immediate positive reinforcement as soon as the change is achieved.

II. Immediate and Delayed Reinforcement

Immediate reinforcers are those we receive immediately after performing a behavior. Delayed reinforcement occurs sometime later, following the performance of the behavior. Immediate reinforcement is much more effective in both changing and maintaining behavior than is delayed reinforcement.

At least three reasons account for the effectiveness of immediate reinforcement. First, as creatures of immediate gratification, most of us like to be rewarded immediately for the things we do. Secondly, as creatures of short memories, most of us have frequently forgotten what the rewarded behavior was if the reinforcement comes too long after its occurrence. Thirdly, since we are active creatures, when too much time elapses between performance and reward, an undesirable behavior which has occurred in that interval may inadvertently be reinforced. A reward given too long after the behavior we want to reinforce may be connected to recent events we wanted to ignore and extinguish.

III. Regular and Intermittent Reinforcement

A regular reinforcer is a reward given consistently each time the desired behavior is repeated. Intermittent reinforcement is given intermittently, as the term indicates, but unpredictably. Since the person being reinforced does not know when it will occur, he keeps on working in hope of receiving the reinforcement.

The regular reinforcer is an effective way of changing behavior; however, it is less effective in maintaining behavior over a long period of time because it satiates in the same way as does the negative reinforcement. If, for example, we give a child M & M candies regularly each time a new behavior is performed, we will eventually satiate him with M & M's and they will no longer act as a reinforcer. A similar thing could happen in the case of our employment. If we were to receive in one lump sum sufficient pay to have adequate means to live the rest of our lives, most of us probably would not continue working as hard as we now do.

Intermittent reinforcement is much more effective for maintaining behavior once it has been established, although less effective in changing behavior. Because the reward is less frequent and given at variable intervals, it reinforces rather than satiates.

Intermittent reinforcement is analagous to a series of immunizations. When a child is initially immunized against an infectious disease by a physician, he or she is given a series of three shots at monthly intervals, which is a regular type of reinforcement.

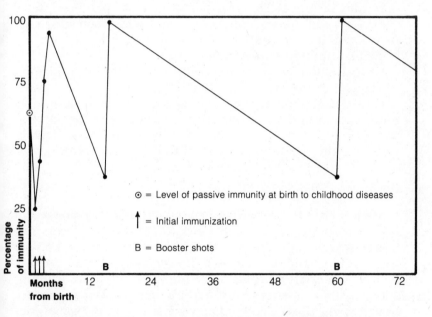

Following the series of three shots, the physician waits one year and then gives a booster shot. The protection for the particular disease then rises to the initial protection obtained from the three shots. Over a period of several years the protection declines slowly. After four or five years the child receives an additional booster shot and the protection is brought again to the previous level. In this way the protection for the disease is maintained with a type of rise and fall curve.

The intermittent reinforcer acts similarly in principle. First, the behavior is established by regular reinforcement. Then, when the behavior is intermittently reinforced, the likelihood that it will continue is increased. Intermittent reinforcement makes it extremely difficult to extinguish a behavior.

Intermittent reinforcement is used superbly in Las Vegas. People from all over the country commute there to deposit and lose their money in the slots or on the tables because of the effective use of intermittent reinforcement. Statistically, not all can go home with the same amount or more money than they brought. The profits and costs of operations must come out of monies people bring with them. In spite of this, people continue to come by the thousands and risk losing in hope of winning that intermittent jackpot.

Unfortunately, intermittent reinforcement of inappropriate behavior occurs continually in families, work situations, and in the general society. If negative behavior is ignored until it is beyond tolerating, the attention bestowed by the angry negative response that finally comes will actually reinforce the person who emitted the negative behavior.

IV. Material and Social Reinforcers

Material reinforcers are the material things that we receive for performing certain behaviors. Material reinforcers are things that we all want or need, things that can be bought with money, and money is a universal reinforcer in our society. Material reinforcers are highly effective in bringing about behavioral change. In many situations we can and do buy the behavioral change that we desire. However, material reinforcement satiates similarly to negative and regular reinforcement. As noted before, if we have sufficient material things—or, the money with which to get them—they, or it, will no longer act as a very strong reinforcer and thus the behavior will be extinguished. For a few people money may become an intrinsic reinforcer even though they do not need the material things that money can buy. However, material reinforcers satiate most people if they are given enough.

Social reinforcements, on the other hand, do not satiate

but are extremely powerful reinforcers. Each of us needs affirmation, acceptance, appreciation, and at least occasional admiration. We want consideration, sensitive response, and thoughtful acts from others. Most of us never get saturated with positive social reinforcers. We like warm words given us and nice things said about us as signs that others think well of us.

Material reinforcers and social reinforcers need to be used in combination. If we lack material things we need and want, then material reinforcement may be a proportionately stronger reinforcer; whereas, if we have many of the material things we want, social reinforcers become proportionately stronger. The hungry want bread, not compliments; as hunger disappears, new social needs become their focus.

The use of reinforcement is not so simple in application. In order to shape each other's behavior to get more of the

---

THE MOST EFFECTIVE REWARDS ARE . . .

POSITIVE. Affirmative rewards say, "You are important to me. I care."

IMMEDIATE. Immediate rewards say, "You come first. I care now."

INTERMITTENT. Intermittent rewards say, "You can be trusted to do what is best without constant supervision. I respect you. I show it when appropriate."

SOCIAL. Interpersonal rewards say, "I value your friendship. I want to be in open, caring, trusting relationships with you."

CREATIVE. Constructive rewards say, "You are always responsible and never to blame. I will stand by your choices which are constructive. I will stand with you while you work out new options when your choices are less than constructive. I am for you!"

---

behavior we want, we must use reinforcers wisely. This is a dynamic, changing, unfolding process, and there is a constant overlapping and integrating of combinations of reinforcers. Combination of two or more or even all eight of the reinforcers discussed in this chapter may be needed in any single situation.

If you want to get more of the behaviors you desire from other people and wish to help them creatively shape their behaviors, use positive reinforcement whenever possible.

If you have to use negative reinforcement, use it briefly and switch to positive reinforcement as soon as possible.

Use immediate reinforcement at all times and resort to delayed reinforcement only if there is no opportunity for immediate reinforcement. Use regular reinforcement if you want to change behavior or get a new behavior started, but switch to intermittent reinforcement as soon as you have even a small amount of the desired behavior since this will maintain the behavior much more effectively.

Use material and social reinforcements in combination.

What About Punishment?

In the discussion of reinforcers, the use of punishment needs careful consideration. Punishment, unlike positive reinforcement, provides an aversive stimulus or unpleasant stimulus. In contrast to strengthening a behavior, as in the use of reinforcers, the goal in punishment is to weaken an undesirable behavior. Although behavior can be changed or weakened by no longer reinforcing it, such a process is gradual and slow. Parents, particularly, often wish to effect a rapid change in behavior, and this can sometimes be brought about by the use of pain or punishment.

Punishment works if it is used properly. However, it has a price tag attached to it, based on the same principle on which the reinforcement principle is based, "You get what you give." People have an uncanny memory for hurt. We remember the times when pain was inflicted on us much better than when somebody expressed kindness and love. The price for the use of aversive stimuli to effect a behavior change is that the process will be returned in kind, either directly or indirectly in a displaced way. But it comes back, particularly when children are punished. They may, in various ways, at other times and places, indirectly strike back at the punishing parent with more unacceptable behavior.

The Reward Rule . . .

YOU GET
WHAT YOU GIVE.

RESPOND TO OTHERS
AS YOU WANT THEM
TO RESPOND TO YOU.

GIVE THE REINFORCEMENT
YOU WANT TO GET.

Since punishment appears to produce immediate results and temporarily changes behavior, the punishing parent is very likely to view it as an effective reinforcer. Often the punishment is a useful experience in releasing tension for the parents, but a useless experience in reinforcing further negative behavior for the child. To model violence is a powerful way to teach a child violent behavior. A coercive child is the frequent product of punitive parents. A friend of mine opened his front door one evening to be met with the sight of his eight-year-old son striking his six-year-old sister. He grabbed the boy by the shirt collar and began immediate spanking. "I'll teach you to hit your little sister," he said. Then he heard his own words. "That's exactly what I have been doing and am doing," he slowly admitted to himself. "I model the very behavior I am trying to extinguish." If punishment is used, mildly aversive rather than brutal stimuli should be used, and these should be applied immediately after the occurrence of the unacceptable behavior. It is extremely difficult to choose a mild consequence, and most people overreact and overpunish. In addition, in order for punishment to be effective, it must be consistently applied every time an unacceptable behavior is emitted. Most of us find this extremely difficult and are inconsistent; consequently, we do not get the results desired but, frequently, the reverse of our hopes.

Choose positive reinforcements first. Resort to punishment only when it seems important to have instant change, such as stopping a child from playing with fire or straying into dangerous traffic.

Experiencing Positive Rewards

Let's begin with you. Your internal behaviors—thinking, judging, and feeling—shape the choices you make. (Then the choices you make and the actions you take shape the future thoughts, judgments, and feelings you carry with you.)

Negative thoughts about yourself, negative judgments about your worth, negative feelings about your behavior all work together to sabotage your growth in assertiveness. Positive statements about your own worth and working abilities can stop your habitual reinforcing of low self-esteem and begin rewarding you for being you. The following steps can aid you in changing this internal triangle of thinking, judging, and feeling negatively about yourself.

STEP ONE: REVIEWING YOUR SELF-STANCE

1. What kind of stance are you taking toward yourself now? Write a positive self-affirmation that reverses each of the following negative statements.

Negative Self-Stance	*Positive Self-Stance*
I keep blowing it.	_____
I always louse things up.	_____
I can't help myself.	_____
I'm afraid to say what I really want.	_____
I feel so powerless around strong people.	_____
I am so stupid when it comes to working through differences.	_____

2. What kind of style do you have for turning positive statements about yourself into negative self-judgments? If you have a skill for turning comments against yourself, and using them to immobilize yourself into a nonassertive position of passive withdrawal, you have responded to the demands of a culture that nourishes negatives and encourages their early learning. Test your skill by reversing these strong traits into negative self-descriptions.

Positive Self-Stance	Negative Self-Stance
I can turn most any situation into a reasonable success.	
I have a knack for making things work out right.	
I can live by my own inner supports.	
I can claim my rights and ask for what I want.	
I feel good about being me no matter who I am with.	
I like differences and enjoy working through them.	

3. Which kind of statement comes easier to you—to turn positive self-statements into negative judgments, or to reverse negations into clear affirmations? If the first comes more naturally to you, then the following exercise is even more useful. If the second, then you're already experiencing skills in self-affirmation. Reward yourself by practicing them daily. You will note that the two example columns given above are each the reverse of the other. Your own written columns should be the two opposite sides of the same traits. Compare. Note similarities and differences.

4. What statements are you making about yourself now? Reflect on your inner messages. Write five negative lines that you habitually lay on yourself. Then reverse them, writing the positive affirmations that you will be saying as you are more assertive:

Negative, Habitual Statements	*Positive, Chosen Statements*
1._____	_____
2._____	_____
3._____	_____
4._____	_____
5._____	_____

Reflect on the statements you use to reinforce your present behavior. Nonassertive statements reinforce nonassertive responses. Nonaffirmative statements reinforce nonaffirmative feelings about yourself and your worth as a person.

STEP TWO: REVERSING YOUR SELF-STANCE

Mental exercises are a necessary behavioral rehearsal which affirm your intentions and explore alternate ways of behaving, but the crucial step is the choice to act in a new way. The following sequence of behavioral steps is a progressive way of decisively altering internal behaviors—thinking, feeling, judging—by choosing new interpersonal behaviors. Select from the following scale those new behavioral steps immediately appropriate and comfortably possible for you. Add a new response each day for one week. Then reflect on your change, noting how feelings about yourself do follow the behavioral change:

1. Select three affirmations about yourself that reverse three of your most painful self-doubts. Write them on an index card and carry them with you, reviewing them at each spare moment.

2. Choose a cue to remind yourself to review your strong points regularly, for instance, at each traffic light when driving, or place a sign on your phone at your desk to remind you each time you make or take a call.

3. Post your affirmations on the car dash, on the refrigerator door, at your desk. When someone asks you about them, simply quote them with no defense and no explanation beyond saying, "I sometimes forget who I am and what I can do."

4. Discuss the affirmations with another person whom you trust. Neither overstate nor understate your strengths. Simply assert your own clear estimate of your ability with frankness.

5. Just before enjoying a favorite reward, relaxation, or enjoyment, review the significant affirmations about your worth, your ability, your gifts. This can come to link affirmation to excitement.

6. When you think affirmatively of yourself in a way where previously you were doubtful, reward yourself with some pleasure, privilege, or excitement.

7. Respond to a criticism with a self-affirmation. When another reports a negative judgment about you, reply, "Thank you for reporting your disagreement with me. I'll think about it. Of course, I know myself to be . . . (the affirmation)."

8. Rehearse affirmations for persons important to you. Write them on cards. Repeat them to enhance your appreciation of the other. Then report them to the other person. Reflect on how this increases your sensitivity to another's worth. Reward yourself for each experience of affirming another's work, gifts, and worth.

Chapter 9.

EMOTIONS
How Feelings Are Formed and Reformed

"That's the way I feel, and I'm not honest unless I do what's true to my feelings. Sorry, but that's the way it is. I feel this job is no good for me. I can't go against my feelings. I'm going to resign."

The speaker believes that emotions are the primary determining force behind behavior, that what a person "feels" is the "truth" by which choices are made and behaviors are determined.

"Yes, I'm afraid of driving in heavy city traffic, but I find that if I go ahead and do things I'm afraid of, the fear gradually goes away. The same is true for anger. A week ago I was so irritated at my boss I felt like I couldn't face him another day. But I need the job, so I decided to act toward him in a positive way no matter how I was feeling. He's treating me with a lot more respect, and one week later I almost like him."

This secretary believes that behavior changes emotions. No matter how she is feeling at the moment, she has found that going ahead and doing the appropriate behaviors will not only make things go better but things will "feel" better too.

Both individuals are right—partially. The relationship between emotions and behavior is intimate and complex. Volumes of written attempts at defining this intricate interconnection mark a central concern of psychology, ethics, theology, and education. In this chapter we will examine this interrelationship and provide insights and experiences for influencing and changing our emotions.

Emotions Are Learned Responses

Walking to school each morning, Ann needed to pass a red house with a picket fence. Inside the fence was a black Doberman that would bare its fangs and snarl at her the whole length of the yard. By the time she would reach the corner, her forehead would be wet and her stomach tight with fear. One morning as she approached the red house, she saw the Doberman clear the fence with a clean leap and chase another dog down the street. For months after that, Ann walked three extra blocks to avoid passing the red house. A black dog followed her in her dreams. Fear shadowed her all the way to and from school.

Ann is a college freshman now. She has long since forgotten about the dangers of walking to elementary school. But last week she was invited to visit her boyfriend's parents. As they drove up to the house, Ann became very anxious. "I'm just afraid of meeting Scott's folks," she told herself. But their warm welcome and the delightful dinner did little to relax her. Her stomach was in concrete knots and she was constantly wiping her forehead anxiously. When she and Scott left, she found herself hurrying to the car and looking at the shrubs along the house suspiciously. As they drove away, she looked back at the red house, puzzled. It reminded her of a place she had been before but couldn't remember. The stimulus of the angry dog at the red house had triggered such intense fear in Ann that the generalization to all red Cape Cod bungalows was a natural defense. Emotional reactions are conditioned readily until they become automatic or habitual responses. If they are conditioned they can be reconditioned; if learned, unlearned.

Yet this process seems uncommonly difficult. We have little immediate direct control of our emotions. Once we have become afraid, we have little direct influence in changing the fear to calmness; once angry, we have no simple direct route for converting the anger to an instant loving response.

Emotions Are Energy Responses

Emotions are energies not under voluntary control. These energies flow through the autonomic nervous system (so named because it is largely independent of the central nervous system's voluntary controls. This is also called the involuntary nervous system because it was thought to be beyond voluntary control from the central nervous system. Now we have learned that this system can also come under voluntary control to a large extent).

Physiological changes, such as the release of adrenalin into the bloodstream, trigger immediate and intense arousal in the autonomic nervous system. These are experienced as emotions and feelings, positive or negative. The emotional content of feelings can shoot up almost instantly as the adrenalin enters the circulatory system. The threat may pass or the behavior change, but the physiological arousal continues for some time, dissipating slowly.

The most effective way to discharge the arousal is through muscular activity and exercise. Carrying the feeling arousal from one situation to the next may not only interfere with efficient handling of the new interaction; it can accumulate and be transformed into frustration and possible aggression.

A favorite exercise, particularly one which utilizes the major motor muscles of the arms, legs, and trunk, can burn off the accumulated adrenalin and reduce tension levels significantly. A teacher who builds up a great deal of tension during a day in the classroom can change her emotions by choosing a physical activity such as jogging or tennis that will dissipate her state of tension as well as improve muscle tone. A musician, when depressed, may immerse himself in playing the piano and find his mood lifted by the music and by the intensity of concentration and muscle movement. Changing behavior can change the emotion and discharge the surplus energy.

In contrast to our limited or complete lack of control over

our emotions, we have complete control over our behavior. It is thus easier to act ourselves into feeling in a new way than to feel ourselves into acting in a different way. We can slowly learn the ability to change our emotions voluntarily, but most of us have the power to begin immediately to change our behavior. This in turn evokes a change in the emotions and feelings we experience.

EMOTIONS	BEHAVIOR
LIMITED CONTROL	COMPLETE CONTROL
INVOLUNTARY AROUSAL	VOLUNTARY ACTIONS
AUTOMATIC RESPONSES	CHOSEN RESPONSES

**IT IS EASIER
TO ACT OURSELVES
INTO NEW FEELINGS
THAN TO FEEL OURSELVES
INTO NEW ACTIONS.**

Emotions—Causes or Effects?

In the suburbs of Chicago, the commuter trains come from the central station engine-first and return to the Loop caboose-first. To sit at the crossing and watch the train being led by an empty caboose on its return to Chicago is to view a parable of human existence.

The executive abilities of the person are in the central nervous system—the brain—that engineers thought and behavior. The many cars that are drawn along represent the broad repertoire of available behaviors. The emotions, which are conditioned by the behaviors, experiences, and situations along the life-route, follow cabooselike, either celebrating the excitement of the journey or riding the rear-end brakes with guilt, anger, sadness, or resentment.

Emotions are feeling-responses to the perceived situations. As such, they are neutral, amoral—neither good nor bad. There are no "good or bad" feelings. Feelings simply are. Values can be attached only to the uses that are made of feelings, not to their content or nature.

Feelings can be an intuitive early warning system in a crisis. Awareness of an impending accident can trigger electrifying fright and avert disaster. But living constantly by emotional energy can keep a person in a low-grade emergency state that exhausts resources and reduces the ability to be resilient. Such chronic hypertension results from a flood of emotional energies which must be brought back under the controls of conscious awareness.

As long as the executive engine directs the train of experiences, feelings enrich experience by adding the dimension of depth and high celebration. When the train is reversed and feelings dictate directions, the choice of direction is left to the lifestyle track or to the moment's inclination as the switch is reached.

If life offers only rigidly prescribed options, like those imposed on a train entering a switching yard, then it matters little if the caboose leads and the engineer is blinded by the long string of cars. So a person directed by feelings may function quite well in a restrictive community where alternatives are limited, choices are few, and virtually all possible options are acceptable. To back into life, feelings first, is no major problem.

Placed on an open freeway, the train can create disaster when tailing its way through traffic. The multiple options of life can thoroughly confuse the feeling-led person unless the ability to be reflective, decisional, and responsible frees him or her to go head first into life. The whole person is the whole train of behaviors, options, and feelings. All parts of the self-thinking, choosing, and feeling are equally important. But the ability to think about feelings and reflect on behaviors enhances choice-making and frees the person to direct his or her life. The ability to be self-reflective about impulses, emotions, and feelings is a mark of maturity.

Developmentally, the human brain is divided into three parts, the archipallium, the pallium, and the neopallium. The first forms the oldest core of the brain stem. It is similar to the brain forms of the lowest animals, including reptiles. The second part, the pallium, is the limbic system, which is common to early mammals. The limbic system is the center of emotions, feelings, and affective responses. The neopallium or the neocortex is the seat of all that is exclusively human in the mind.

The Archipallium—the primal brain, similar to a reptilian brain stem—the action part of the brain

The Pallium—the more developed mammalian brain, common to lesser animals—the emotion part of the brain

The Neopallium—the most developed brain, the neocortex with ability to think rationally, reflectively, personally—the reasoning-thinking part of the brain

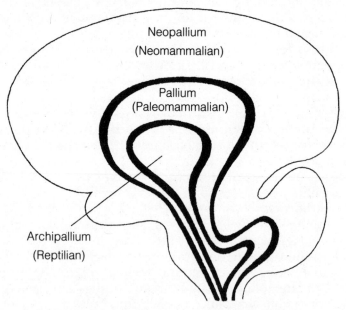

LEVELS OF THE BRAIN, SHOWN DEVELOPMENTALLY

The interconnections between the gray matter of the neopallium and the spirals of the limbic system bring logic and emotion together. Through this interconnection we can volitionally affect behavior and bring balance between thought and feeling, between emotion and action.

Living primarily from the limbic system occurs for persons who are emotionally overconditioned so that feeling overrides thinking and dictates behavior. The person who behaves strictly on an emotional level has chosen a lower level of intellectual functioning than he or she is capable of.

Living totally from the neocortex, on the other hand, requires the suppression or isolation of emotions until the person is no longer aware of them. Behavior becomes mechanical, with little humanness. Computerlike, the individual processes thought and behavior without the feeling richness of the limbic system's effect.

The whole person uses all of his or her capacities in a smoothly balanced physical and emotional health. Such a balance, or homeostasis, integrates brain functions into a harmonious whole. The primal skills of instant reflex are valuable in averting danger, such as touching an exposed electrical wire which could give a severe shock. The skills of the limbic system offer an emotional radar to the world and stress readings on the self which inform the person about the positive or negative character of situations within or without. The thinking skills of the reasoning brain provide the insight and understanding to integrate both of the above with the values, beliefs, and intentions of the person.

Emotions—Reliable or Unreliable?

Emotions are notoriously unreliable. Since they are conditioned responses they do not change readily. Once learned, they recur repetitiously without fail. They are unreliable because they are conditioned to an earlier stimulus which seldom occurs again in even an approximate form. A fragmentary similarity can trigger the entire behavior. A red house may release an old flood of feelings. Fear, helplessness, resentments that were appropriate responses to the Doberman of long ago still dog an adult's steps in inappropriate ways.

A neurosurgeon, Wilder Penfield, demonstrated how emotional "mind sets" are permanently retained in the brain. When operating with local anesthesia on a partially exposed brain, he gave minute electric stimulations to various areas of the cerebral cortex—the gray matter. (The brain has no pain sensation.) As an area was stimulated, the patient would recall very early childhood experiences describing these in vivid detail and with the intense emotions experienced at age two, three, or four. Memory patterns laid down within us are probably never forgotten. When a stimulus is provided, parts of that early experience flash into awareness.

Emotions are a naturally reliable recorder of experience, but a notoriously unreliable distorter of recalled experiences. Shame and guilt, for example, edit memories thoroughly. Unacceptable actions and their painful consequences are so thoroughly reworked that the person's recall may only slightly resemble the original embarrassing bind.

When a nonspecific stimulus is provided, it will produce an old emotional reaction (a dated emotion) which may well be totally inappropriate and unreliable for the present situation. Actually, the adult is feeling toward his or her adult relationship in a way decided by a four-year-old child, thirty years before. So, trusting the feeling, he makes a crucial choice based on an emotion conditioned in a spiteful brat who wants candy at any cost.

Jill, fifty-five, has been married thirty-five years. Within the last five years she has become an alcoholic. Her alcoholism prevents her from caring for the home, doing the cooking, and keeping up with the laundry. Heavy arguing and blaming are distancing Jill from her husband. After a number of hours of therapy the following story unfolds:

Jill grew up with a coercive, controlling, authoritarian father. Children were to be seen and not heard. When Jill's father spoke in his deep burly Irish voice, she fearfully obeyed in passive compliance.

Jill's father died when she was sixteen. She had never

related to her father as an adult. She had experienced only a father-child relationship, not a father–adult daughter relationship. At twenty she married a man of Irish descent, burly, with a deep voice and an authoritarian manner. For thirty-five years, Jill would freeze, withdraw within herself, and rarely if ever make a response to his criticism. As the years passed, she accumulated more and more hostility and anger toward her husband but could not understand the reason. Eventually, this resulted in so much emotional distress that she began to seek relief by having an occasional drink before her husband returned home from work. Over the next five years this increased progressively, and by the time they went for help she was inebriated nearly every evening before dinner. As therapy progressed, she began to identify that she was trying to escape from the distress that occurred whenever she felt like a child being controlled by an angry father. Obviously she was no child, and certainly this demanding control was intolerable, but she knew of no way to retaliate except by drinking.

During therapy, she complained that her husband would question her intelligence to do the simplest things. For example, when he would ask, "Why do you put so much soap in the laundry?" she would feel intense hostility but would give no response. From his point of view, he was not questioning her ability, only wanting to talk about the appropriate amount of soap.

Jill chose not to converse about the content of his questions, but to withdraw at the tone of voice. Later she got relief through the use of alcohol, which unfortunately led to her addiction.

Jill was conditioned to a specific type of resonse as a child. When confronted with a similar stimulus to her father, that is, her husband, who possessed some of his characteristics, she responded as to her father. Such conditioned responses can result both from internal events as well as from external. The internal events of one's thoughts, imaginations, and fantasies, sometimes act as stronger stimuli than the real situation. Negative emotions are particularly unreliable because many of the early conditioning experiences were negative ones.

Emotions—Generalized or Specific?

We experience the same type of emotions for vastly different situations. We may have great anxiety prior to a test. We may have anxiety when awaiting the return of a long-absent parent, child, or lover. We have similar emotions when we have a physical illness or when we fear an impending catastrophe. The internal physiological changes are the same in both situations.

Fred developed severe postoperative bleeding after major surgery, and lost so much blood that he went into shock. He felt his pulse accelerating; his mouth became dry, his chest tight, his palms clammy; and he was very short of breath. An immediate transfusion diminished some of the symptoms. After further surgery, the bleeding stopped, his fears subsided, and his physiological responses returned to normal.

Several years later, while visiting his parents, he perceived that they continued to have a great deal of conflict and there was much arguing while he was present. It was much like their fighting when he was a child and constantly feared they might divorce and abandon him. Several days after returning home he became extremely nervous and tense while trying to enjoy a leisurely evening. His heart began to beat wildly; his chest became tight, his mouth dry, his palms sweaty; and he felt short of breath. He felt he was going into shock as he had after surgery years before. Certain that he would die, he called his therapist in panic. He could think of no reason for the shock reaction since he had been feeling perfectly well. Obviously he was not hemorrhaging. Slowly he was able to recognize that seeing his parents in their continual state of conflict had been a "catastrophic" stimulus which triggered a major physiological reaction reminiscent of the physical emergency. Emotionally, the impact of the two experiences was so similar he could not differentiate between them; however, the causes were quite different. The physiological shock was a dangerous situation; the emotional panic was not immediately life-threatening. Specific emotions can be generalized to many similar or only slightly similar stimuli. The nonspecific feeling responses of fear, anxiety, anger, or resentment quickly generalize to associated stimuli.

Emotions—Blind or Insightful?

Emotions are reactive. They are responses. They are independent of the perceptions, views, and thoughts of the seeing, perceiving, hearing, thinking, judging, and reasoning skills of the neocortex, the reason-center of the brain. The emotions emerge from the limbic system's response to the signals, signs, and situations perceived.

Emotions are sometimes called a sixth sense because they can be an accurate intuition of what is taking place in another or between others. Such hunches are only inklings of what is happening and must be checked out carefully with the other. Intuitions are highly valuable, but they are best when balanced with careful thinking, reflecting, and cautious inferences.

Emotions, when exaggerated and inappropriate to the situation, can overwhelm and stop all senses from functioning. Hearing, seeing, smelling, touching, and tasting—one or all—can be shut off. Emotions are then both blinding and blind.

"Love is blind." So are the other major emotions when escalated beyond balance. In fact, love is considerate, caring, self-sacrificing, and compassionate. It is not love that is blind, but the manic emotions that are often confused with love. The manic acceleration of any primary emotion can excite the person beyond sight, or sound, reception. The excitement of intense emotion can block out all objectivity. Imperfections, limitations, contrasting lifestyles become invisible. Relationships that from an objective point of view obviously could not succeed seem perfectly logical and inevitable. Tremendous differences between likes and dislikes, among beliefs, hopes, and goals, seem utterly irrelevant. We are similarly blind to the reality of situations when we are angry, depressed, frightened, or overwhelmed by any other emotion.

Sally is an attractive young lady in her twenties, with warm, intense, and impulsive responses. Repeated conflicts with her supervisor have further conditioned her feelings and emotional reactions. In a constant state of tension, she finds that her problem-solving abilities are hampered and her work performance is less than desirable. Her supervisor has pointed this out frequently, and she feels constantly picked on. One unfortunate day when the supervisor offered a bit of criticism, she became extremely angry, striking back with her best verbal aggression: The supervisor punched her out on the time clock, and placed her on suspension.

After driving for about twenty minutes, she found herself on an extremely busy highway in an unfamiliar area of the city. Totally confused, she pulled off the road to reorient herself. She suddenly realized that she had driven five miles in the opposite direction from home, run four stop signs on the way, was involved in two near-accidents, and at the moment of coming to her senses had nearly run a red traffic light while a large truck was crossing the intersection. Her excessive emotional reactions had so blinded her that she had behaved in an almost disastrous way.

Emotions—Rational or Nonrational?

Frequently people make statements like "I feel like that was a wrong decision." This is not only inaccurate, it is untrue. It is not a feeling that is being reported, but a judgment. Feelings or emotions do not make decisions; they do not have intelligence. Decisions are a function of rational, intellectual thinking—cognition. Certain of our decisions may result in a comfortable or uncomfortable feeling, and on this basis we judge them to be right or wrong. The feelings give us emotional data, but insight and understanding are thoughts. We read our emotions and then conclude with a decision. Feelings are simply used as a guide to our conclusion, and do not present the conclusion itself.

Good problem-solving thinking seldom occurs when we are in a state of emotional upheaval. Since our emotions are integrated in the lower part of the brain and not in the grey matter, they are an adjunct to logical reasoning. Emotions are similar to the physical reflexes that are integrated at the spinal cord level. They occur instantaneously, without rational control. They do not weigh and cannot predict how a person will respond if they take control. Particular emotions occur simply because they have been conditioned to accompany certain situations and not because they result from an intelligent reaction.

Anita, a middle-aged married secretary, was recently assigned to a new supervisor. Although he was considerably younger than Anita, he was friendly, warm, and supportive. Within weeks, Anita was intensely attracted to him and her strong warm feelings led to an illicit affair. After several weeks of rendezvous, he terminated the relationship, and she felt extremely hurt and exploited. She responded with furious anger and aggressive behavior. This further disrupted their relationship and made her miserable, depressed, and nonfunctional. Ignoring these feelings only increased them until she was totally out of control of her emotions and finally sought therapy. Anita's emotions had no intelligence to foresee the chaotic and miserable situation she would get herself into because of her strong, warm feelings for her boss. The emotions were simply conditioned in response to the positive and flattering stimuli she received.

Emotions Are Valuable and Invaluable!

Although our emotions are unreliable, nonspecific, blind, and stupid, they are an equally important part of being human. As a warning system, they are physiological responses to life situations that may signal an impending disaster, and they may avert intense distress. As a caution system they can stimulate pain and internal unease. Pain is a gift. Pain is a sign that something is dysfunctioning within the person. Pain is a valuable invitation to check out what is wrong and work out a more productive life-enhancing way of being.

To deny or suppress feelings in an attempt to get rid of the distress results in denying our humanness. The economy of our humanness has a deep need to be balanced, and we may distort or juggle the figures in a vain effort to make them come out. This will not make the bottom line in our internal budget balance, however. When we deny emotions and force them under the surface, they inevitably erupt at another place, perhaps at a considerable distance. Suppressing angry emotions may eventually make us depressed months or years later. We may not be able to make the right connection and never understand the process by which we are depressing ourselves.

Handling negative emotions seems particularly difficult because the distress that results makes it hard to see the value of pain and suffering. It is helpful to remember that we can use pain and suffering to become better people or bitter people. Pain is more often an asset than a liability. Pain rarely if ever kills anyone. The pain of a heart attack, for example, does not kill the patient. In reality, it may save his life by causing so much distress that the patient seeks proper medical help and thus survives what might have been a fatal heart attack. It is the cause of pain that destroys, not the pain. This is true in both the physical and emotional realm.

Unfortunately when we hurt emotionally we too often curse the pain rather than look for the source so that we might get at the root of the problem and find a way of getting healing. It is not the pain but the lack of healing which destroys people. The human being can tolerate much repeated pain from surgery as well as illnesses as long as there is healing. If progressive infection occurs, the individual will not long survive as healing cannot take place in the face of uncontrolled infection. Emotional pain is caused by inappropriate behaviors and inappropriate conditioning to others' behaviors. Emotional pain destroys the meaningful and fulfilling interpersonal relationships that are needed for persons to be physically and emotionally whole. If we continue inappropriate behaviors in spite of the emotional distress warnings, relationships can die. When emotional pain is taken as a signal of relationship stress and the inappropriate behaviors are changed, the relationship is frequently much better and stronger than before the hurt. When properly tended, a cut will heal with scar tissue that is stronger than the skin around it. A well-healed scar will rarely come apart as easily as the adjoining skin. So it is with healed relationships.

Mabel is a 27-year-old graduate student whose husband is suing for divorce. He has a pattern of constantly harassing her over any available issue for weeks at a time. One day not long ago he refused to agree to return money that she had recently loaned him from her inheritance. Extremely upset, Mabel dipped into intense depression. The following day she cut all her college classes. This gave her more time to brood over how she was being exploited. Her depression increased, triggered suicidal thoughts, and further immobilized her. Two days later she became irritated at her emotional bender and frustrated with her tendency to be enslaved by her emotions. Once she began to look at her behavior, she realized that she was compounding her misery by staying home and ruminating. She decided to go to class whether she felt like it or not. Back at college, her teachers and friends who knew about the difficulty she was facing in her marriage were supportive with positive reinforcements. She began to realize that people do care and her emotions began to lift. Her depression dissipated and her husband was no longer in control of her feelings. Mabel used her emotions as a warning signal to focus her attention on her behavior. Discovering that she did not need to be enslaved to her emotions, she behaved assertively in spite of negative feelings. As she began to behave differently, her thoughts turned from self-pity to interest in life. Her emotions were rechanneled from negative to positive; her depression lifted. By the end of the day she felt much better about herself.

142

USING EMOTIONS AS A BAROMETER OF
INTERNAL STRESS/EXCITEMENT

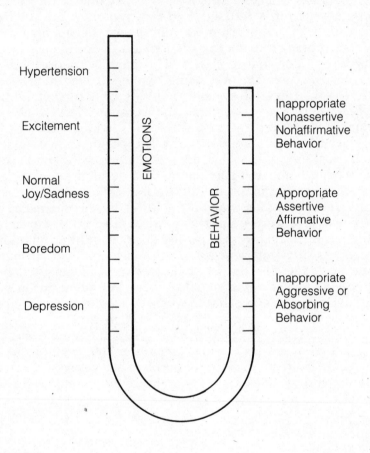

Feelings are an early
warning system . . .   . . . that . . .   . . . behaviors need to
                                                    be changed.

Using Emotions Constructively

We can use our emotions as we use the barometer. The mercury in the barometer flows freely up and down as the atmospheric pressure changes. We don't complain about the readings it gives us nor do we curse the weather. When the barometer goes up the weatherman predicts good weather. When it goes down he predicts inclement weather. He may issue cattle warnings and highway warnings for the protection of animals and people. Heeding the barometer can be lifesaving. If, however, there is an obstruction to the free flow of the mercury to give us feedback concerning the weather, we are left to second-guess the elements.

If we claim our emotions, develop a sensitivity to them, and read them as they begin to change, they can be a great asset. We do not need to focus attention on the emotions and try to suppress them when they are uncomfortable. Since emotions are conditioned responses to behavior, we need to let changing emotions direct us to look closely at our behavior.

We need to ask ourselves, "What am I doing that is causing me to feel so bad?" If we use our emotions as an index to internal health, they can quickly call attention to behavior which can be effectively changed. The earlier we intervene in our behavior, the less strongly will our emotions be conditioned and the more quickly they will dissipate; the more rapidly we will find relief from the distress.

Emotions are an invaluable barometer, an indispensable early warning system to indicate inappropriate behaviors so that we can intervene where we have control and make life more meaningful, enriching, and fulfilling.

We can develop our skills in differentiating between behavior and emotions by learning to recognize and read our emotions accurately. This is a primary step toward changing those inappropriate behaviors which trigger negative emotions. In this way, our emotions can become even more valuable than the barometer. One cannot change the weather. One had better not change the barometer.

But we can change our behavior, which in turn alters our emotional barometer positively rather than negatively. Thus, heeding our emotional barometer can give us the ability, influence, and power to make life more enriching.

Feeling Skills Exercise

Just as ideas need to be expressed clearly and accurately, so feelings need to be described simply and precisely. To be accurate in identifying feelings is a necessary step toward changing the behavior that is evoking the emotion. Consider the following:

Inaccurate Ventilation		*Accurate Description*
Command:	"Shut up!"	"I hurt too much to hear more . . . I'm too angry to go on talking with you now."
Questions:	"Is it safe to be driving so fast?"	"I'm afraid of doing sixty on ice."
	"Why did you do that?"	"I'm angry at your behavior."
Labeling:	"You are really an insensitive clod, you creep."	"I feel rejected and insulted when you ignore me."
Accusation:	"You don't care about me at all."	"I feel unloved and lonely when you talk only to others at parties."
Sarcasm:	"You know so much about everything, don't you?"	"I resent your self-confidence."
Judgments:	"You're terrific."	"I really like your sense of humor."

Inaccurate Ventilation	Accurate Description
"You bore me to tears."	"I resent you when you run on and on."
"You talk too much."	"I feel angry when I'm not equally heard."

Based on the preceding examples, write a "V" for ventilation before each option that expresses feeling in an inaccurate way. Place a "D" in front of those that describe the feeling clearly.

_____ 1. "Button your lip. You've made enough trouble for one day."

_____ 2. "I'm really annoyed at this constant hassle between us."

_____ 3. "Can't you let me have a moment of peace, for once?"

(1 and 3 are angry commands in statement and question form, but no feeling is stated.)

_____ 4. "You've monopolized the conversation all afternoon."

_____ 5. "You drive me bananas when you run on and on."

_____ 6. "I'm beginning to resent your need to talk so much."

(4 and 5 are judgments and blaming statements, not a report of feelings experienced.)

_____ 7. "I feel that you think only about yourself."

_____ 8. "I don't feel like you ever hear a word I say."

_____ 9. "I'm irritated when you show little interest in my excitement."

(Watch out. 7 and 8 are deceptive. The word *feel* is used wrongly. The speaker is calling a hidden judgment a "feeling," but no true feeling is expressed as in 9.)

_____ 10. "I'm so depressed that I flunked my algebra final."

_____ 11. "I'm a born loser; I just blew my final test."

_____ 12. "I feel that was the lousiest test ever written."

(11 and 12 are judgments of self and of an object. They ventilate but do not describe.)

_____ 13. "I just don't feel capable of leading a group discussion."

_____ 14. "I'm just not adequate to function as a leader."

_____ 15. "I feel that everyone cares about me as a group member."

(14 is tricky. It is like the described feeling above, but is actually a judgment, as is 15, which judges the group's caring. If the speaker had said, "I believe that the group feels caring," he would have been making an actual affirmation of belief.)

Book Three.
HERE AND NOW

Becoming assertive.
Becoming affirmative.
Exercises in asserting.
Experiences in affirming.
Experiments in being
positive and powerful.

Chapter 10.
BECOMING AFFIRMATIVE
Exercising and Experiencing Affirmation

"I'm fed up with your criticizing me; I've had enough for one day; now get off my case," I protest to my wife (I've only made two wrong turns, and hit six out of ten available chuckholes).

"That sounded very much like a criticism of me," she replies. "I'm not on your case. You have a knack for interpreting anything I say in a negative way."

"Ridiculous. I know when you're needling me. I can get the point. Cut it out."

"So I'm pricking your inflated ideas of perfection, eh? Come on down to size! You're overcrowding our Datsun."

Who's negative? Husband, wife, and the atmosphere surrounding them both. Review the four responses. Each statement is a negative comment on what preceded, a negative criticism of what is, and a negative command about what should be. The three negatives stimulate equal negations in the other.

Such a spiral of nonaffirmative behavior is so universal among humans it is "the law of negation." Negatives elicit negatives. Nonaffirmation triggers nonaffirmation. Unappreciative attitudes and nonaffirming behaviors are uncommonly common in the human community. They appear early in life in the first training parents offer. Learned misbehaviors, as first behaviors, are learned as soon as an infant becomes effective in crying.

Learned Misbehavior

I appreciate you by being happy with you, prizing and respecting who you are and what you are. I appreciate me by being happy with me, valuing and delighting in who I am and what I am.

The law of negation tragically intervenes.

I can learn to be appreciatively happy with you. Or I can learn the art of blackmailing others by acting and being unhappy.

In a world of negations I learned to be negative.

I have learned to be unhappy with you and unhappy with me. I have learned to be unloving.

I learned to be unhappy now in the hope of being happy later.

I dread obesity to motivate me to eat responsibly.

I fret about unemployment to coerce me to work conscientiously.

I condemn myself harshly after a "failure" to prevent me from repeating it carelessly.

I pout when I feel hurt to make the other person feel guilty and miserable.

I get depressed when someone important to me is unhappy to show him or her I feel with and so love him or her.

I get impatient and irritated with my children to make them obey immediately.

I make myself unhappy to get things I think will make me happy, or to prevent things I think will destroy my happiness. The end result, either way, is that I am unhappy here and now in the hope of being happy there and then. But two negatives do not make a positive.

Unhappiness is praised as sensitivity, caring, affection, concern; it masquerades as all the virtues.

One's seriousness about life is not measured by his or her capacity to be unhappy. Caring is not measured by how unhappy one can become for others. Wisdom is not proven by the degree of pessimism and despair one shows. To love you is to find joy in your presence, to be happy with you, to be thankful for you, to appreciate you.

Live with Affirmation

Affirmation can be a lifestyle. A positive position toward relationships provides a stimulus for increasing trust and then reinforces that trust. Powerful as such a way of being with others is, it is often lost by default because the social environment may be largely negative, the natural reinforcers around us are commonly negative, and the haste of living demands the instant results that negative responses to others will temporarily provide.

The self-defeating effects of a negative life-position are easily seen. For example, a self-rejecting person expects to be rejected by others and will tend to reject others. As a result of his rejection, they will likely respond in the same rejecting way, thus confirming his/her original expectations.

A self-accepting person, in contrast, will expect acceptance from others and will tend to accept other people. They in turn are more likely to be accepting in response. His/her original expectations are reciprocated, and thus confirmed.

Such self-fulfilling prophecies, once learned, can become a continuing lifestyle. The negative stimulus offered others produces a negative response. These negative consequences become a new stimulus to evoke further negative responses. The identical process can be reversed. Rather than a negative snowball of rejection stimulating rejection, which in turn creates even greater rejection, positive behaviors can evoke more positive behaviors. Affirmation can elicit more affirmation. Appreciation invites similar appreciation.

The law of "stimulus-response-consequences" can work for us or against us. In fact, it is working for us or against us in our relationships whether we choose consciously and overtly or covertly and largely unconsciously. If we take an affirmative stance toward life, choose to value persons ultimately, and are unquestionably for others, we will find ourselves prizing people, caring for people, understanding, supporting, empathizing, and loving them for what they are. Such a stance can result from an aware choice to value others as oneself. It may be an unaware life-position that reflects deeply held values that appear as habitual behavior, as an unconscious response, as automatic valuing of self and other in normal life situations.

To live with affirmation requires internalizing affirmative values, learning affirmative behaviors.

Lead with Affirmation

Assertiveness, no matter how brilliantly exercised, is effective in creating balanced relationships only as it occurs in a context of affirmative regard.

The driver of a stalled car with an automatic transmission requested a push from a Good Samaritan motorist. "I need to be pushed at thirty miles an hour for the car to start, understand?" he asked. The other nodded, climbed into his car and started the engine. The stalled driver waited for the gentle bump of the cars connecting bumpers, but felt nothing. So he looked back. To his horror, he saw the other car coming at him at thirty miles an hour!

Rear-ending another who asked for a gentle shove is a common interpersonal experience. To impact another without first linking emotional bumpers wrecks relationships. Collusion must connect us when we exert our power against each other or collision will push us out of shape.

Along the freeway, I witnessed a friendly attempt at helping that was inflicting repeated whiplash. The driver of the pushing car kept losing contact, then speeding up to nudge the other again and again. The smooth interchange of power was broken and the jolt was bone-wrenching.

When two persons confront, the interface can be bruised and traumatized unless contact is consistently maintained. Rapport is all-important. The balance of affirmation-connection with assertion-exertion of power is the crucial element in expressing interpersonal energy. Here are eight parallel principles for effective interaction.

Loving Must Come before Leveling

Leveling with others is offering a gift of openness. To love another is to open yourself to that other. But not all openness is loving. In fact, little openness is authentically honest.

To say, "You drive me up a wall with your gossiping about your family and your constant critical carping about your mother; you are so judgmental you make me sick," is open but not honest. The dishonesty lies in the blaming, judging attitude and the assigning of responsibility for my equal anger and self-righteousness to you.

To say, rather, "I am put together in such a way that I come unglued inside when I hear someone describing his family in largely negative terms and I want to be your friend on a different basis; let's talk about you and me rather than people not present," is a more honest statement that describes the behavior objected to without adding my negative conclusions and value judgments. Loving another is respecting his/her right to his/her perceptions and feelings and my equal right to my own. Loving another is reporting my objections in an objective way rather than an objectionable way. Loving must precede leveling.

Love that values the other as worthful can balance and buffer feedback to a more useful and admissible form.

Effective relationships depend on one's ability to accept others as worthy of love, respect, and appreciation and to communicate agreement and disagreement levelly. This frees the relationship so that demands and expectations can be expressed and negotiated. If I love you I can tell you my "truth." Because I love you I will share my "truth."

First I will love you; then you may be able to hear my "truth" and respond clearly with yours.

Trust Must Be Experienced before Risk

I am trusting you when I am aware my choice to be open with you could lead to either happy or unhappy results, to a closer relationship or to rejection and distance, and yet I am open anyway. Though I realize that the consequences of my choice are dependent on your behavior, still I risk openness.

Trust and risk go hand in hand in building relationships. As trust is gained, more risks can be taken. Each additional risk is at one and the same time an extension of the trust experienced and an invitation to even greater trust. Greater trust is a base for further risk. Step by step, risk follows trust, trust grows from risk. But trust is primary. Risk that has no trusting base may be courageous, but it must soon be rewarded with trust or the relationship falters. Trust welcomes risk. The more trust, the more the other is freed to be spontaneous, to be openly vulnerable, to be with few defenses.

AFFIRMATION IS PRIMARY

ASSERTION IS SECONDARY

Love **before** leveling.
Trust **before** risking.
Care **before** confronting.
Support **before** criticizing.
Understand **before** interpreting.
Empathize **before** advising.
Affirm, **then** assert.

Caring Must Be Expressed before Confrontation

Experiencing growth with others requires the capacity to truly care for the needs of others as well as to confront them on the issues in focus. When a basis of caring exists, differences can be faced, frustrations examined, creative solutions explored. When I truly care about you, I will offer confrontation because it will contribute to our relationship and perhaps to each of us as persons. Self-care, relationship maintenance, and care for the other are three valid reasons for confronting. But each of the three must be balanced by equal caring for the other, the other's needs and relationship, and the other's unique ways of expressing caring in return.

A caring relationship is a special kind of relating that is more than accepting, appreciating, understanding, hearing, feeling with another. All these are expressions of awe, respect, approval which may or may not express caring. The crucial issue in caring is that movement by which life maintains and enriches itself, which we call growth.

To bid another person to grow is to care for that person. To invite the other to become what he or she truly is and can be is to care for him or her.

To care is to experience the other person as a part of me, as like me, as similar enough that I can identify with his or her perceptions, feelings, and choices.

To care is also to experience the other as distinct from me, as unlike me, as a truly separate other. So I will respect his or her differentness, and not violate the uniqueness that is a precious part of the other's personhood.

To care is not to impose my directions for growth, but to model, affirm and to be my own directions. To care is to be guided by the other's direction of growth, although I will choose my responses, I will select my behaviors. Such caring precedes and undergirds all growth-producing confrontation. It is the basis on which a frontal disagreement can be shared effectively with another.*

Support Must Be Given before Criticism

Communicating negatives about another person's behavior is much more useful in a relationship of stated acceptance than in one of possible or even implied rejection. If it is clear that you are unquestionably *for* another, you may be able candidly to examine difficulties *with* that other. When you support another as a person, you can more freely report your objections to his/her behavior.

---

*Mayeroff, Milton, *On Caring* (New York: Harper, 1971).

The most difficult part of receiving criticism is that the critic is so easily seen as a judge. Criticism is useful when it is an expression of support and directed toward increasing another's sense of well-being. Criticism is useless when it serves only "to get it off my chest," or "to put the shoe on the other foot," or "to lay the blame at the other's doorstep." To be useful it must contribute to the relationship, not ventilate free-floating emotion or violate the other person's integrity or worth.

Support is a clear report that the relationship is valued and the information about to be shared is an expression of that estimate of worth. Support is a contextual statement that we "are speaking in a context of respect"; it clarifies the content statement that "the content of our conversation is a sharp disagreement which deserves our debate."

Support is talking "about" while criticism is talking "to" the issue in focus. Support is a form of positive meta-communication, that is, communication about our communication. It is offering instructions on what I want from my words with you as I try to express what I mean in my words to you.

Frequently people object, "But I'm not feeling supportive when I'm irritated. I feel critical and to offer support then is phony, it's artificial, it's even dishonest. I'm honest with my feelings. I tell it like it is. Let the chips fall where they may."

This is the all-too-human problem of mistaking the part for the whole. At the moment I may be blinding myself to the importance of our relationship and blocking out how deeply I do care about continuing contact with you. I am willing only to see my frustrated side and to speak for my irritations, expectations, and demands. To offer these criticisms with no report of my support may "feel honest" at the moment, but it is at best a half-truth. The other half is in the unspoken support. To speak for the whole self is authenticity; it is power; it is asserting and affirming.

Understanding Must Be Offered before Interpretation

Interpreting another's behavior in your own words and according to your views is useful as feedback only after understanding has been expressed and established between you. To repeat another's point of view without adding interpretations, analysis, or personal bias is the most direct way to check out understanding for yourself and to communicate it clearly to the other person. But parroting the identical words in instant replay has little value except in situations where the other is extremely anxious. Paraphrasing the identical thoughts in brief summary using the same emotional content and a similar tone of voice can clearly indicate that you are hearing with an inner ear and understanding the meaning. Whether or not you agree with the point of view is open to later interpretation and reinterpretation, once a basis of understanding has been built in this moment. A past foundation of understanding is important, but each encounter must be grounded in freshly expressed understanding of each other to clarify or reconnect the relationship here and now.

Eye contact is the most genuine means of expressing understanding. A sudden break in eye contact is often a signal that the person has just felt misunderstood. (You may have understood only too well and responded too accurately for the present trust level.) Reflecting what you have just heard can test whether a base of understanding exists and further statements of your interpretation can be offered. When the open glance appears in the eyes signifying that rapport is restored, exploration may be resumed.

Empathy Must Be Shared before Insight

Accurate empathy is demonstrated through open sensitivity to what the other is experiencing and then communicating that understanding in a way that resonates with the other.

Charles Truax and Robert Carkhuff researched the therapeutic outcomes of the counseling practice of psychotherapists of many different theoretical schools of thought. They discovered three basic ingredients common to all persons successful in helping relationships, no matter which theory or what techniques were used. Effective people-helpers exemplified these traits: (1) *Accurate empathy*. They were sensitive observers of the other person's feelings and views and able to express them in ways that accurately reflected the other. (2) *Nonpossessive warmth.* They were accepting persons who saw the other as a person with human potential and of worth totally apart from any evaluation of his behavior or thoughts. (3) *Genuineness:* They met the other person in a direct encounter, on a person-to-person basis, without defensiveness or a resorting to a façade or retreat into a safe role. They could continue to be present no matter what threat or demands were faced.*

Lead with affirmation. Affirming each other's worth firms up the relationship with the solidarity required for either strengthening the existing ties or creating new ones. Affirming the other as a person confirms the relationship that exists between you as mutual humans, the trust that unites you as vulnerable humans, the respect that protects you from the irritations of being close to others.

---

*Truax, Charles and Robert Carkhuff, *Toward Effective Counseling and Psychotherapy* (Chicago: Aldine, 1967).

Effective Affirmative Feedback

The goal is to offer the maximum amount of information with a minimum of threat to the relationship.

Nonaffirmative Feedback	*Affirmative Feedback*
Focus feedback on the person. Criticize the person; generalize criticisms to cover the whole personality.	Focus feedback on the behavior. Criticize the behavior in question, not the person.
Offer feedback with judgments. Label the person as good or bad, right or wrong, nice or rude. Make conclusions; risk inferring intentions and motives.	Offer feedback with descriptions. Report observations only in clear descriptions with as little bias and as few conclusions as possible.
Express feedback as qualities. Point out the qualities disliked. Use adjectives which name traits and characteristics: "You were an obnoxious loudmouth."	Express feedback in quantities. Use terms denoting more or less; use adverbs which relate to actions: "You talked considerably more . . ."
Report feedback on history. Relate it to abstract patterns and indistinctly recalled incidents; give yourself time, do not deal with conflicts until feelings cool.	Report feedback on immediacy. Relate it to specific situations, preferably in the here and now. Report as soon as appropriate. Do not become historical or hysterical.
Give feedback as advice and answers. Give pointed answers to the other's problems; tell him/her what to do with the data offered.	Give feedback as alternatives. To increase another's options is to enrich. Giving ideas and information leaves the other free to decide.

Nonaffirmative Feedback	Affirmative Feedback
Give feedback in amount available. Focus on value to giver; say what you need to say for your own release; say it when it suits you.	Give feedback in amount useful. Focus on value to receiver; give what is useful without overloading; be sensitive to other's optimum time to receive.
Focus feedback on why. Keep asking, "Why?" Judge the other's values; question his/her motives; confront with the "truth."	Focus feedback on what and how. What-how-where relates to observable, changeable behaviors. They offer growth and hope.

Exercising Affirmative Feedback

Reflect on a relationship which is uncomfortable to you now and which you would like to see change. Write notes on the kind of feedback you could offer the other person that would be sharply focused and clearly affirmative.

1. Focus feedback on the behavior (offer support):

_____

_____

2. Offer feedback with neutral description (and respect):

_____

_____

3. Express feedback in "quantity, not quality" terms (with caring):

_____

_____

4. Report feedback on immediate situations (with under-standing):

_____

_____

5. Give feedback as alternatives (with empathy):

_____

_____

6. Give feedback in amount useful (with trust):

_____

_____

7. Focus feedback on what and how (with love):

_____

_____

Compare your feedback notes with the two columns on the preceding page, item by item. Did nonaffirmative behaviors creep in? Edit your responses to express clear affirmation.

Chapter 11.
BECOMING ASSERTIVE
Exercising New Understandings of Assertiveness

"Now that I've learned how to be assertive, no one walks over me," Jeff reports, grinning. "I can outmaneuver anyone trying to put one over or to put me down."

Jeff is a quick learner—of skills and techniques. His mother keeps him under constant surveillance, even though he's twenty-six. "You came in late again last night. That's the third time this week," she says, accusingly, over breakfast. "Right," Jeff replies. "I've been late the last three nights. I'm glad you care about my getting enough sleep."

Jeff knows how to agree with any criticism offered, and still go right on doing whatever he wants. He can "yes, ma'm," or "yes, man," any objections, no matter how accurate they are. "I just admit that the logic they're laying on me is flawless, the predictions of failure are perfect, and I do it my way."

Jeff has learned to outmanipulate his manipulators, outconning even the most cunning—some of the time. But one of the inevitable facts of life is that manipulators get manipulated.

Being assertive is no gift to yourself or to others if it offers only the skills of outsmarting controlling people, of one-upmanship on critics, cynics, or cranks.

Assertiveness becomes a creative way of insisting on the best for yourself when it is equally insistent on the fulfilling of the needs of others. Being genuinely assertive will not make people dislike you, parents resent you, family avoid you, or colleagues stay away from you. Assertiveness is expressing your feelings, at the same time equally respecting the feelings of others. Assertiveness is requesting your wants and equally honoring those of people important to you.

You Choose the Restaurant

Alex is a seafood addict. Jan and the kids enjoy it too, but not for every meal they eat out. On those rare occasions when someone in the family insists on something else, Alex does a pouting routine until the food arrives; then he becomes the complete food critic, service critic, etiquette expert, until everyone is miserable.

As Jan becomes assertive, she can say, "Alex, you're free, of course, to eat wherever you like tonight. I'm going to an Italian restaurant. The kids can pick whichever they prefer. Then let's have dessert together at the ice cream place."

Or she may want to assert an even more risky solution. "Alex, I want to have dinner with you, and I'd like for each of us to have equal turns at choosing restaurants—you, me, Jerry, Ann. And wherever we go, I want to make it a happy occasion for us all, so no criticism of food or service, agreed?"

The process of selecting a restaurant is an accurate test for any family's problem-solving ability. The behaviors used in avoiding making the choice, or in criticizing the other's taste, frequently show off the worst in the family's decision style, fight style, compromise style and their collective acid indigestion (of the emotional stomach, if not the overstuffed one).

A nonassertive response, "I'll swallow my feelings," stores up frustration. "I'll go along with you and eat the cuisine you choose, but I won't like it. I'll stomach my irritation, but I'll hate it."

The nonassertive person is all abdomen. From early years he has learned to ingest frustration and to try to digest it alone. Interpersonal problems get internalized as if they were personal problems (which they then become). Slowly the accumulation of frustration builds until it amounts to a time bomb.

Such behavior insures an eventual aggressive release. Accumulated frustration is eventually acted out whether it is done passively ("I'll just show you how much I'm hurt by giving you the silent treatment") or actively ("You make me so angry. You don't care about me at all; all you want is your way in everything"). The aggressive personality stomachs little. Chronic, lifelong hyperacidity has been learned from childhood, and caustic words supported by explosive actions may be triggered by almost any frustration.

That Was the Last Straw

Like the proverbial camel, the nonassertive person collects straws of irritation until the load is truly backbreaking. The aggressive person, in contrast, is constantly near the point of spinal collapse and only a straw or two is sufficient to crack the emotional sacroiliac.

Each person has his or her own frustration threshold, a point at which tolerance ends and temper is activated. Low-control systems, like the aggressive person, reach this threshold quickly. High-control persons, like the nonassertive person, can absorb great amounts of frustration over long periods before the threshold is reached.

The nature of these controls varies widely.

1. *Conscientious controls* are constructed of strict moralisms, which teach that all open expression of frustration is evil, tasteless, inexcusable, sinful, unforgivable, evidence of low worth—all of the above, only one of the above, or something even more insidious than the above.

2. *Apprehensive controls* are forced in by a threat environment in which high fear, anxiety, guilt, shame, and loss of face are continuously reinforced by threats of being found out, driven out, shut out, or ignored.

3. *Restrictive controls* are built in by years spent in a very narrow environment that modeled only one kind of response to frustration, permitted only that kind, and rewarded any other kind with such withering extinction or wounding punishment that the person has no awareness of alternative behaviors, and no ability to even imagine trying something else.

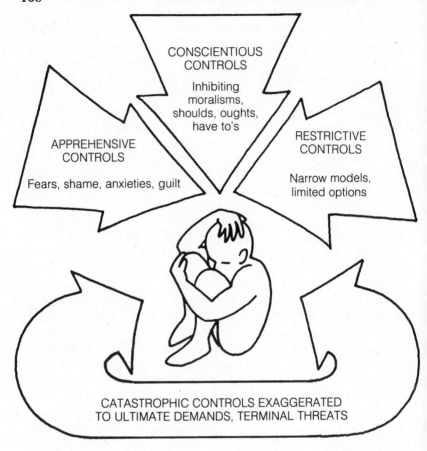

CONSCIENTIOUS
CONTROLS

Inhibiting
moralisms,
shoulds, oughts,
have to's

APPREHENSIVE
CONTROLS

Fears, shame, anxieties, guilt

RESTRICTIVE
CONTROLS

Narrow models,
limited options

CATASTROPHIC CONTROLS EXAGGERATED
TO ULTIMATE DEMANDS, TERMINAL THREATS

4. *Catastrophic controls* are created by combinations of several or all of the above. The key difference is that the control forces are exaggerated to impossible demands and the threats are stated in terminal language: "I'll kill you if you slam that door once more," or, "It will just kill me if you ever talk back to me like that again." Once the control has been worded in ultimate language, the escalation of anxiety and guilt can effectively block out consideration of alternatives or experimentation in options that involve even the slightest risk. (If a catastrophic monster lurks outside the door of change, even opening it a crack is out of the question.)

Assertiveness Ends Controls

Assertiveness renders controls obsolete. These ineffective behavior patterns can be discarded as soon as more effective responses are learned. Controls are useful intermediate steps a child learns in order to manage the flood of opportunities and options that pour in during the first five years of life. If these controls are maintained for the next fifty years, they are stifling and stultifying.

Not controlling but channeling is the mature solution. Assertiveness is not a means of childlike overcontrolled or childish uncontrolled behavior. Assertiveness is adult channeling of drives, needs, wants, and dreams to reach the goals in the most effective way at the most appropriate time possible.

Channeling requires not an impenetrable wall to responses, but clear boundaries and sharp goals. Not containment through overcontrol, but discharge through directed flow. Not bottling up of energy in nonassertiveness, nor explosion of energy in aggression, but focusing of power, coordination of effort, cooperation of energies exerted in assertive and affirmative purposefulness.

Anger energies, for example, can be controlled in denial and disowning, or they can evade the controls by being recycled as "feeling hurt, concerned, suspicious, distant," ad infinitum, all of which slowly poison the self and the relationship.

In contrast, the anger energy can be immediately expressed aggressively in an explosion of rage. The absence of either controlling or channeling of the anger allows it to diffuse generally into persons and relationships with little impact.

Channeled anger focuses the demand while balancing it with the needs of others in relationship; asserting power while affirming mutual interrelatedness and interpersonal respect.

As channeling emotions, energies, and expectations becomes more effective, controls atrophy and fall away. As the person becomes more confident of his or her ability to express power impactfully, the need for controlling becomes less and less. The goal of maturation is channeled power, expressed assertively and affirmatively, confronting the issue in view and caring equally for the persons involved.

High Control—No Control

High control of response to frustration has a breaking point. As frustration mounts, the nonassertive behavior becomes less and less effective at containing the mounting anxiety. Then the response swings all the way across the scale to aggressive outbreaks.

Each person has his or her own boiling point (the boiling point is the temperature at which a liquid bubbles and turns to vapor and gas). To pursue the metaphor, some persons have nerves of steel (iron's boiling point is 3000° C.) and can withstand emotional heat that would reduce others to a steaming rage. The nonassertive person with a high boiling point may be able to absorb frustration indefinitely with no verbal or emotional loss of cool.

Other persons maintain a boiling point close to their normal functioning temperatures. As with ether (which boils at 34° C.), little heat is required to convert them to volatile gas. Such an instantly aggressive response pattern can boil over in anger at slight provocations.

High-control people, with temperaments of iron, and no-control people, resembling volatile gases, live painfully and exploitively alongside each other in most communities. Nonassertive persons with consistent controls inhibit their responses almost automatically. Aggressive persons with little control ventilate their emotional pressures spontaneously. Each kind finds the other intolerably passive or unbearably coercive. Even though one trusts controls and the other resists controls, they are more alike than different. Each has his or her own authority problem. The true opposite in behavior is channeling the energies creatively in affirmative-assertive behaviors.

When the Mouse at Last Roars

The nonassertive person, no matter how high the boiling point, has his/her moments when emotion begins to vaporize explosively, or when anger begins to simmer dangerously.

Frustration tends to accumulate in geometric progression. We may begin the day with a normal emotional temperature. The first frustration hits, and rather than dealing effectively with it, the problem is avoided, internalized, and converted into a kind of frustration fever. Up one degree. As the day progresses, problems multiply, are denied, swallowed, converted to emotional energy—but not degree upon degree. Each frustration doubles the preceding addition: one, two, four, eight, sixteen, thirty-two, sixty-four. Frustration follows frustration, doubling, redoubling, and doubling again. The geometric sequence is inevitable if we choose to use the same escape response. Emitting the same nonassertive behavior doubles the frustration previously felt.

An astoundingly trivial frustration that impacts us when the frustration fever index is already at 64 can double the pressure to 128 and cause controls to rupture with an aggressive outbreak, contaminating the relationship. A small amount of frustration resulting from an inconsequential problem stimulates an unmanageable load of frustration if we are already functioning at a high level. This type of frustration accumulation is a painfully familiar experience to most of us. It is particularly frequent in relationships between parents and children. A parent attempts to be patient with his child. Rather than responding simply and immediately when the child's behavior begins to turn slightly unacceptable, the parent overlooks it: "It isn't worth bothering with; in fact, he's acting quite cute." As the behavior becomes progressively more unacceptable, the parent avoids intervening by postponing a proper type of action. As the day progresses, the frustration accumulates (geometrically). Finally the child performs a very insignificant negative behavior that results in the parent "blowing his stack": "I've had enough of this carrying on today. That's it. You go to your room and stay there until you can be good." The last behavior the child emitted may have been unimportant; it was simply "the straw that broke the camel's back." The child recognizes that the punishment is hardly fitting to the "crime." It simply appears inconsistent to him since he has kept no account of the many minor irritating behaviors which the parent was accumulating as anger-energy building to a fever pitch. Now that the inappropriate parenting exists as a barrier, the conflict between parent and child will continue to mount unless proper restitution is made.

The parent has hit his ceiling of irritation tolerance. Most people have a surprisingly consistent limit of frustration tolerance and, when that limit is exceeded, will blow a "head of steam" that is very disruptive. Each person's level of frustration tolerance is unique to him or her. One person may have a frustration level tolerance of 16; another, 32; and another, 64.

In any event, when the person walks around with frustration near the limit of his tolerance, a minor stimulus will effectively produce a frustration exceeding his tolerance level and lead to aggressive behavior. Not only does each person have a different limit of frustration tolerance, but each of us has a different limit of frustration tolerance under different conditions. If we are in good health and everything goes well, our limit of frustration tolerance may be considerably higher than when we awaken in the morning with a headache after a poor night of sleep. In any event, when we hit our limit of frustration tolerance, we blow out of control, skipping right over the assertive behavior and on to the aggressive.

Assertive Channeling

Assertive behavior, in contrast to nonassertive behavior, is not problem-escaping, but problem-solving behavior. The assertive person meets problems head on, channeling assertive and affirmative energies toward a resolution of differences and a reconciliation of the persons who are differing. This mode of behavior takes both courage and focused power since so much of our social reinforcement opposes it.

If we act assertively and we get rejected or hurt, we are immediately negatively reinforced because rejection (being ignored) and actual physical injury result in pain from which we would rather escape. Consequently, these negatives reinforce us toward the nonassertive or aggressive behavior

NONASSERTIVE RESPONSES	AGGRESSIVE REACTION
Frustrations slowly accumulate . . .	The frustration limit is reached.
One . . . Two . . . Four . . .	Suddenly aggressive behavior erupts.
Eight . . . Sixteen . . . Thirty-two . . . Sixty-four . . .	
Nonassertive behavior is consistently emitted. Frustration is constantly accumulated. The anger temperature rises . . .	Explosion, acting out; then guilt, shame, and intense reversion to Nonassertive behavior styles.

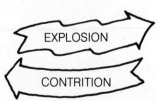

EXPLOSION

CONTRITION

which most of us have learned all too well. Immediate negative reinforcers are extremely strong reinforcers and can inhibit the expression of assertive responses. In addition, occasional negative feedback acts as an intermittent reinforcer for the old nonassertive behavior. When these two extremely strong reinforcers act in combination, one must be quite assertive in order to maintain affirmative behavior. On the other hand, these same two reinforcers can act in directing the behavior toward the aggressive side if one's previous conditioning has been more aggressive than nonassertive.

Understanding Assertiveness

Reflect on an assertive experience you have had. Then list below the kinds of behavior you emitted in that experience.

Problem-Solving Behaviors:

1._____

2._____

3._____

Vulnerable, Risk-Taking Behaviors:

1._____

2._____

3._____

Affirming-Respect Behaviors:

1._____

2._____

3._____

Think back . . .
As I dealt with the problem, rather than considering escape . . .

———— (1) . . . I took the risks of rejection, blame, hurt.

———— (2) . . . I acted in a way that showed high regard for self and other and my respect for our relationship

Assertiveness Exercises

Visualize yourself in the following situations as a behavioral rehearsal. Cover the responses in the right column, and in the appropriate space provided in the left write your own ideas of nonassertive, assertive, aggressive responses, and a fully assertive and affirmative response. Then uncover the right column and compare your response with the printed one.

SITUATION:

You're traveling with your family. You and your wife had coffee at the motel, and the kids had snacks. At 10:00 A.M., your wife and daughters insist on stopping for breakfast. You want to wait and have an early lunch so you can get to the motel early and have a swim. They spot a restaurant and insist on stopping.

Nonassertive Norm:

You stop, silently. Inside, you order nothing, offering no comment. Back in the car, you say: "Now you all won't want any lunch and I'll have to do without. You didn't hear me voting for that greasy spoon! Boy, they sure took their time in serving; they should have tipped us."

Assertive Alan:

"I'd like to save time today so we can swim tonight. I vote to drive one more hour and have an eleven o'clock brunch. How do the rest of you vote?"

Aggressive Alex:

"All you people want to do is stop and eat. I'm fed up with shooting the day in restaurants. No way am I going to stop anywhere until lunch. Now just chew your gum and dry up!"

Affirm-and-Assert Andy:

"Driving makes me hungry too. I want to stop in at least an hour. I'd vote for an eleven o'clock brunch so we can get there an hour sooner and spend more time in the pool."

SITUATION:

Your car air conditioner is dripping cooling fluid from under the dash and losing its power to beat the heat. You've had it repaired once; then a week later you discover a very slow leak. After the mechanic has checked it again, he reports the fluid is from the previous break and pronounces it O.K. You are still unsatisfied and unsure that it will not give out on your vacation trip across the desert.

Nonassertive Norm:

You shrug, accept his opinion, pay for the check-up, then go to another shop, critically cut up the first mechanic and buy a second check-up, which you also begrudge.

Assertive Alan:

"I'm not satisfied that the air will hold for the trip. I'd like for you to dry it off with a cloth and run it a bit more. Or, could you have one of the other mechanics here give a second opinion?"

Aggressive Alex:

You bite back your disbelief for a moment, then decide to get it off your chest. "I'm not paying for anything you've done today unless you come up with a better story than all that. Now, I want it fixed and fixed right or I'm taking my business elsewhere for good."

Affirm-and-Assert Andy:

"I recognize the leak was in an impossible place to get at; I appreciate your taking a second crack at it. I still don't trust the machine. I'd like for you to rub it dry and give it one more once-over before I take it across the desert."

SITUATION:

The authoritarian English teacher has just returned your paper, which you consider among your most creative, with a large C on the front. A firm believer in rote memorization and accurate reply of content, he apparently hasn't appreciated your freedom to express yourself in nontraditional ways. To say you are disappointed is an understatement.

Nonassertive Nan:

You swallow your disappointment and chide yourself for even imagining that he might find one of your creative styles satisfactory as an assignment. You resolve to offer him his stodgy party line.

Assertive Ann:

"I'm quite disappointed with your rating for my paper. I thought a novel approach might rate an A. I've enjoyed doing it. I'd like your feedback."

Aggressive Angie:

"I can't believe you gave me a C for my best paper. Obviously you couldn't have read it. I'm not about to write the traditional junk that others turned in and were rated with an A."

Affirm-and-Assert Andrea:

"I'm aware I took a bit of creative license in doing the assignment. I think it came out quite well, and I'm disappointed with the grade I received. I'd like a chance to talk with you to receive your feedback on my creative work. I'm sure I can learn a good deal from you. And I hope to persuade you to respect my work more, too."

Exercises in Saying No

The ability to say no is an indispensable part of maturity. Learning the art of a clear, firm negative is learning the necessary skill of taking responsibility for your own life, schedule, and priorities. To test out your freedom to let your yes be yes and your no be no, work through the following exercises carefully, choosing how you would say no.

SITUATION ONE:

One of your coworkers who habitually imposes on others drops by your office and asks to use your car over lunch. He borrowed your car once before, did not offer to pay for gas, and a scrape appeared on the back fender. "I'm in a real bind," he says. "I have to have a car for a very important meeting. It's only twenty-five miles downtown."

Your response:

SITUATION TWO:

You've planned to spend the weekend camping with your wife and son. Thursday afternoon your supervisor lays a special request on you. He needs a job completed and in the mail by Saturday noon. "Help me out this

Your response:

time. I'll give you a break in picking your vacation time or anything else I can do to help. o.k.?"

SITUATION THREE:

You've just gotten home from a hard day. Your wife will be coming from her job in a few minutes. Your brother calls asking you to come over quickly and help him unload the lumber for his new garage. "Leave a note for your wife. You can eat later. o.k.? You've promised to help me on this, remember? See you in ten minutes, o.k.?"

Your response:

SITUATION FOUR:

"We really need you on the youth committee for the coming year," your pastor says. "You are well liked by all the high schoolers, and you will have a good staff to lean on. The kids deserve your help. If you don't, I don't know who will." You hear his argument, but you want the extra time for a continuing education course you've been planning to take for a full year.

Your response:

After you have said no in your most characteristic way, compare your responses with the following models. Your example may be better. The criteria for a clear no are: (1) Is it direct in refusing the request without rejecting the person doing the requesting? (2) Is it nondefensive in affirming your freedom to choose and your priorities in choice-making, without excuses, evasions, or apologies? (3) Is it affirmative of both self and other in relationship as the option is being refused? The following are one person's *no* responses to compare with yours.

Situation One: "No, I don't want to lend out the car. I'll drive you to the Budget Rent-a-Car over on Westmore. It's only seven dollars a day for the first hundred miles. Or there's an eleven-thirty train that will get you downtown in thirty minutes." (Suggesting options is a way of affirming interest in the others; it can be considered an invasion of the other's freedom to work out his or her own choices.)

Situation Two: "I appreciate the scheduling problem you are having, but I've already reserved that time to be with my family, and it's not negotiable." (Affirming your priorities for family time with no hesitation and no defense gives a clear signal.)

Situation Three: "I'm glad you remember that I promised to help you on the project. If you ask me a day ahead, I'll do my best to be there, but tonight is out."

Situation Four: "I'm glad you thought of me and trust me for such a job. Sometime I'd like to be part of it. For this year, no. I want the time for several projects of my own."

Reflect on your answers. Rewrite them as you see ways to be more direct, nondefensive, and affirmative. Look for opportunities to try out a clear no each day. (You can rethink and accept the request later if you wish.)

Chapter 12.
BECOMING OBSERVANT
Modeling and Learning from Models

"I've been dating Judy seriously for three months," Greg says. "I thought we were really becoming important to each other. Then last Saturday, I blew it with her.

"I finished my work at school, and drove out to the park where Judy was throwing a weekend party for her school staff. I got there just as things were breaking up and she gave me the brush-off.

"I said, 'Hey, dear, I'm finally here.'

"She said, 'Sorry, Greg, too late. We're just packing up. I've got three errands to run. Then I'm coming back here to hunt for a contact lens I lost in the cabin last night. So I'll be too busy to be with you like we planned. Call me next week, o.k.?'

"I haven't called her. She was giving me an invitation to clear out and get lost. I got out!"

Greg responded with virtually the only conflict response in his repertoire—passive withdawal. If he had several optional behaviors equally available he might have been much more effective in continuing a really important friendship. Now a week of passive avoidance has terminated the relationship, temporarily—or perhaps permanently.

Judy's point of view may have been: (1) "I'm really disappointed Greg missed the fun. I'm embarrassed the party broke up sooner than expected, and I'm frustrated that I've three jobs to get done and a lost contact lens to find. I'll level with Greg. He's tired too from a hard day's work. I'll encourage him to go home and get some rest." (2) "I wish Greg could sense how bugged I am that I've been stuck with all these jobs after the party, and I hope he offers to help. Everyone else has cleared out and left me with the work. If he stays to help I'll know he must really care about me. I won't ask, of course. That would spoil everything."

Greg's automatic assumption was: (1) "She's giving me the brush-off. I'll take the hint and get out of her hair." If he had a more versatile behavioral repertoire, he might have concluded: (2) "She's tired, and I'll bet she'd like some help but won't ask for it. Especially from me, since I wasn't in on the party and didn't help make the mess. I'll offer to lift half the load. Besides, all I want is to be with her tonight." Or he might have sensed something more affectionate: (3) "I'll bet she's embarrassed that the party she invited me to has petered out before the time I agreed to come. She's probably worried that I'm upset. I'll let her know I don't care; in fact, I'm delighted everyone's gone and I can be with her alone."

Greg did blow it, but not by coming late. He blew it by not coming through with a better option than passive silence and pensive withdrawal.

Greg's problem is an impoverished repertoire of conflict behaviors. He knows how to be nonassertive—his father modeled that. All three fathers, to be exact. They packed up and fled when the feelings got tense. Greg knows how to be aggressive. His mother was a super model from whom to learn aggressive control of others and absorbing love styles. These two behaviors are about all Greg has in the pocket at the moment. He's looking for alternative models, but most of the options he sees conflict with the overlearned styles of avoiding or eradicating conflict that are his parental inheritance.

A Museum of Models

A person's behavior potential, like a family museum, is composed of the collected ways of responding to threat which have been learned through life. Individuals cannot behave in a way outside their behavior potential. They use the behaviors available for the situation as they perceive it. The more richly stocked the museum, the more versatile and free the actor who owns it.

If I say to you in a commanding tone of voice, *"Machen Sie das Fenster auf, bitte,"* how will you respond? Anxiously—thinking that I am showing signs of being disoriented? Suspiciously—suspecting I am about to do something erratic? If conversing in German is a natural part of your behavioral skills, you will respond *"Ja, ein Moment, bitte."* and move toward the appropriate object. If I keep repeating the phrase and no understanding is communicated, frustration will mount.

Such advice, orders, instructions, or criticisms are frequently heard as a foreign language. But modeling provides immediate communication.

If, as I repeat the German phrase I go to the window, open it and repeat each word with an appropriate gesture, you will immediately add a sentence of German to your behavioral repertoire. You will no longer be limited solely to English.

Language behaviors, communication behaviors, conflict behaviors, affection behaviors are all learned from models we have observed and interactions we have witnessed. These are often incorporated as a complex of behaviors learned from parents or siblings. Like parent, like child.

In a Colorado campground, I watched the manager cutting up a long log for firewood. Balancing the log across a rock, he put his left foot on the log to stabilize it and applied the chain saw. At the other end of the log his four-year-old son stood with his left foot on the log. As the father cut off a short piece, he would step off the log, advance it a short length, replace his foot. The boy, identical to his father, mimicked the model in every detail, even to biting his lower lip. Like father, like son.

Modeling is one of the fundamental ways by which new behavior is learned and old patterns of behavior are modified. Observing another person's actions for the purpose of learning a desired behavior, either intentionally or fortuitously, is one of the first learning processes of early childhood.

Helping my friend Lyle change a tire, I was fascinated by

his 18-month-old son's flawless imitation of his father's behavior. While his dad hammered out a dent on the hub cap, little Allen found a hammer and went to work on the front wheel cover. The dad took a wrench to tighten the lugs. The little guy found a similar wrench in the tool box and tightened the valve stem. His behaviors were exact replications of his father's modeling. He observed, he repeated it, he got reinforced for it by his father's chirping encouragement. He expected further approval so he repeated it again. And again.

HAVE YOU EVER SAID . . .

"Don't do as I do; do as I say."

? ? ?

EMPTY WORDS!

People behave the behavior they have seen modeled.
They **do** do what you **do**.

HAVE YOU HEARD IT SAID . . .

"What you do speaks so loud
I can't hear a word you say."

? ? ?

As a child matures, the mimicking operation can be internalized into thought processes so that the learning can be achieved not only from direct experience but also through observation of other people's behavior and the ensuing consequences. Life is much too short, and the cost of error much too high, to attempt learning all that is needed from direct firsthand experiencing.

The ability to recognize and carefully select the appropriate models of useful ways of responding to others is the true sign of wisdom. The more capable a person is of learning from models, the more rapidly growth, maturation, and effective management of conflict are achieved. The ability to learn from observation as well as participation increases the possibility of rapid and effective growth. If I see you respond in a firmly assertive and caringly affirmative way to a tense moment of conflict, I learn to do the same by watching your exercise of love and power and admiring the consequences. In fact, some of the most effective learning comes in observing another's model. When the observer is not in a threat situation, openness and receptivity are not obstructed by intense anxiety. When involved in direct encounter, the tension of interaction can make learning difficult and retention of the experience almost impossible.

Expanding Your Repertoire

Three key elements shape the learning process in most situations: experiencing, expectancy, and reinforcement.

Experiencing: An alternate model must be observed in clear demonstration that makes it easy for the observer to identify himself with the one modeling the new response. To truly experience an alternate model is to be able to say, "Hey, I can do that too." "Sure, I can be like that if I want to, and I do want to."

The other week I was watching a master teacher field student questions. A woman in the back row raised an involved question that was hard to follow. "I'll bet you're right," the teacher replied, "but I need to hear you say it once more to make sure I'm really with you." Beautiful—he expressed affirmation and respect; he asserted his need for her to repeat the statement. And both flowed so genuinely the woman went on to clarify her point even more as he brought out her best. I learned from that teacher in watching him respond with automatic respect to a confusing statement that could have been avoided or evaded.

Last week a student of mine reported, "You won't remember this, but your best model of being affirmative and assertive happened in an incidental way. I overheard you say you had just put two hundred pounds of salt in your Datsun trunk to give traction on ice. Another professor said, 'That's not necessary. If your little car is as good as mine, it has better traction without the extra weight. Act smart and get rid of it.' And you replied, 'So that's how it works out in your Mazda. I'm finding the Datsun holds the road better with more weight.' No rancor. No defense. Just respect for the other's point of view and affirmation of your own."

His hunch is correct. I don't recall a word of it. And that's how modeling is most effective. I watch for models of clear affirmative-assertive relating, I learn from them, and I seldom go back to say thank you. Now he has modeled that for me in a very rewarding way. I'm learning as much from him as he from me.

Expectancy. Every model observed kindles a set of expectations in the viewer. Every model incorporated into the self is absorbed with a set of positive or negative expectations about its probable effect on self or others. We are not machines who flash reflexively from stimulus to response in all situations without an intermediate choice-making process. Between the stimulus and the response stand expectancies.

Technically, an expectancy is an estimate of the probability that a particular reinforcer will occur following a specific behavior in a given situation. Simply stated, expectancy is the state inside the person that leads him or her to expect certain outcomes of choosing behavior A over behavior B. Expectancies are learned from early childhood on throughout life, but many of the most habitual are those learned most early. They worked then; they don't fit an adult now.

"If I treat you well, you will treat me well."

"If I smile when angry, you won't know I'm mad."

"If I admit I am angry, I am owning I am in the wrong."

"If I give in immediately, you will feel guilty and give in, too."

"If I say 'I'm sorry,' you will have to forgive me."

"If I am always nice, no one can be nasty to me."

"If I say I feel sick, others will have to care for me."

"If I am always helpful, I can earn others' love."

"If I come on strong, others immediately yield."

"If I stay on the offensive, I never need to be defensive."

"If I can't do something perfectly, I won't do it at all."

"If I show any sign of weakness, I will be scorned."

"If . . ." ad infinitum, ad absurdum.

Expectancies are an incredibly mixed assortment of hopes and fears, of internal instructions and warnings. Unexamined and unedited, they can immobilize a person in a moment of decision. When rational abilities are frozen in ambivalence, the decision will most likely be made by the emotions of the limbic system or in panic by the primal reflexes of fight or flight.

Reevaluating expectancies from an adult point of view, reasssessing their accuracy for predicting the outcomes of behaviors, and readjusting our predictions of success or failure to be more realistic and consistent is what education, therapy, and maturation are about. A whole system of effective psychotherapy focuses largely on altering expectancies. Rational Emotive Therapy teaches with the ancient philosopher Epictetus, who, in the first century, wrote, "Men are disturbed not by things, but by the view which they take of them." As Shakespeare said through *Hamlet,* "There's nothing either good or bad but thinking makes it so."

Expectations function commonly in self-fulfilling prophecies. Anticipated outcomes trigger behavior which evokes the expected response from others. The person reports the desire for a constructive outcome but meanwhile predicts disaster in a destructive conflict. The expectancy shapes the response. Stimulus, filtered by expectancy, emerges as a negative response.

Experiencing alternate models requires the expression of expectancies immediately associated with the new model. As the expectancies are altered, the model is assimilated and the new behavior becomes possible.

"I'm going to have to drop out of seminary," John reports. "I've used up all my financial resources. My dad owes me six thousand from my mother's estate, but I'll never see it."

"Let me hear how you would go about asking him for a thousand dollars to finish out the year," I suggest.

"I can't ask him. He'd kill me if I demanded anything of my mother's. Besides, his new wife has claimed it all."

Note the catastrophic expectation. When I challenge it, he reports on his father's violent treatment of his mother, his sister, himself, all of which occurred fourteen years ago.

I then model an assertive and affirmative way of requesting the financial aid. "Won't work," he declares. "Either he wouldn't listen or he'd throw me out." The model is appropriate but not useful until expectancies are tested and redefined. I invite him to play his father; I become an assertive son. After modeling three possible encounters, we reverse, and he tests out his ability to be both fair and firm. Suddenly he breaks into laughter. The old expectancies are gone and the memory of how certain he was that his father would annihilate him now evoke surprised delight as he recognizes his own power to be affirmative.

Reinforcement: Expectancy is the reward we anticipate; the reinforcement value is the reward we really get. Observing a model for behavior and experiencing it vicariously become effective as we alter expectancies and then select the reinforcement we hope to achieve.

Internal reinforcements of delight in affirming our own worth and exercising our own power are a rich reward for acting in a more just way.

External reinforcements of new justice, integrity, harmony, or mutual respect with others are the payoff for using more assertive/affirmative models for interpersonal transactions.

As a new model for behavior is observed, ask, "Does it accomplish what the person is striving for? Is it socially harmonious and responsible to community living? Did the person feel good about it? Would I feel excited about such an outcome in my life situation? Is this a possible way for me to behave more powerfully?"

As a new model is attempted, there is every likelihood that it will receive some negative reinforcement from others. Their surprise at your new assertiveness, their anxiety at needing to respond to you in unaccustomed ways, their frustration at no longer being able to take advantage of you in previous ways, or their insecurity in any disturbance of the status quo may one or all motivate overt (open) or covert (disguised) negative feedback. Initially, you will need an outside source of feedback—a stable reference point—such as an understanding counselor, friend, or pastor who can offer support during the change process. Internal reinforcement is equally valuable. To give yourself strokes for each new assertive behavior, and double strokes for each new affirmative way of responding to others can offer reinforcement sufficient to stabilize yourself through unsupportive situations.

Bob had a long history of acting nonassertively. He had been rehearsing an assertive set of behaviors to use with his boss. One day, as his boss became very aggressive, Bob risked asserting himself and refused to accept the barrage of constant critical attacks. He informed his boss he did not appreciate being yelled at nor did he care to absorb unnecessary anger, since it upset him and reduced his work efficiency. His boss was taken aback, and lamely retorted that he was too sensitive and was wearing his nerves on his fingertips. Then he blusteringly told Bob to leave for an hour or two and cool off. Bob didn't know how to respond to this and felt defeated. He regressed to his old nonassertive behavior.

Totally confused by his first attempt at assertiveness, he hesitated to share this experience with his wife immediately upon returning home. Later when he told Sue what had happened she instantly became upset. His nonassertive behavior in the past had been a constant irritation to her. She attacked him for being so nonassertive and letting his boss walk over him again. In addition she berated him for being so nonassertive that he waited to share the story. Sue was reinforcing the very behavior that she found unacceptable. Resenting Bob's nonassertive behavior, Sue modeled aggressive blaming. Rather than modeling assertive behavior and reinforcing him for his attempts to change, she modeled aggressive behavior which is equally nonassertive and further inhibited his willingness to risk again.

Deciphering Complex Models

Most models are complex combinations of behaviors, and the student who indiscriminately incorporates whole chunks of a teacher's behavior frequently swallows the good with the bad, or ingests the bad and passes the good by. The faults which stand out may be copied, while the strengths which are less noticeable are overlooked.

In order for the observer to be able to learn most effectively from the model, he must be able to discern the stimulus, the logical expectancies, and the relevant behaviors which the model performs.

The observer will not learn the matching behavior if he does not clearly recognize or sharply discriminate the specific features of the model's behavior. If a model seeks to teach effectively, the modeling must be made so specific and simple that the observer can grasp it. Too often persons want children, employers, friends, etc., to learn from complex modeling that is beyond their ability to understand all in one piece. So the attempted teaching goes "over their heads," and the teacher gets angry at them for not catching on, for not paying attention or for being "stupid." (The model is the ignorant one.)

Successful modeling requires responses that are clearly discernible. Obvious distinct and simple responses are more readily learned than subtle or sophisticated responses which must be extracted or teased out from among numerous other responses in which they are hidden. In complex learning, such as playing the piano, a model-teacher will insist the student follow each step meticulously until the process is learned well. Only after the correct fingering is mastered will the teacher permit shortcuts. This is not done because such meticulous behavior will be necessary after the basics are learned, but rather that the student needs to be meticulous in order to learn them. Such stepwise progressions are inherent in educational systems. Children first learn how to add whole numbers before the addition of fractions. The alphabet is mastered before words; words are read before phrases.

Modeling explicitly seems so difficult because once something is learned it seems so simple. Certainly everyone else should be able to understand it instantly. We forget that it once was complex and confusing for us too. The person may have had poor learning experiences in the past that make it difficult for him or her to learn things as quickly as expected. Or previous learning may be the exact reverse of what is now being modeled.

In such cases the model must examine his or her own behavior to discover what is being done incorrectly rather than project the blame on the other person. Most therapy is relearning. Most growth is relearning. Most anything can be learned if a model is willing to begin at a student's level and teach step by step.

The emphasis to this point has been on positive aspects of modeling. However, modeling unadaptive behavior may be just as effective as modeling adaptive behavior. Because of this, responsible persons who prize community choose behaviors which will not model the type of interactions not worthy of being mimicked. Desirable, adaptive behaviors which create community and offer optimal conditions for living together are a gift of loyalty to all humankind. Combining modeling with consistent reinforcement is probably the most efficacious method of transmitting, eliciting, and maintaining socially concerned response patterns for building the community of man.

The question is not whether we want to be models for others; we are models. There is no means of avoiding it. We cannot not behave, just as we cannot not communicate. The question is, "How effectively are we modeling behaviors we want our community to learn?" We can do it very effectively when we understand and apply the principles diligently. We will be much less effective if we do it by hit and miss. In fact, we may inadvertently model precisely the behavior we don't want others to learn.

The effectiveness of modeling is beautifully expressed by Dorothy Law Nolte:

Children Learn What They Live

If a child lives with criticism, he learns to condemn.
If a child lives with hostility, he learns to fight.
If a child lives with ridicule, he learns to be shy.
If a child lives with shame, he learns to feel guilty.
If a child lives with tolerance, he learns to be patient.
If a child lives with encouragement, he learns confidence.
If a child lives with praise, he learns to appreciate.
If a child lives with fairness, he learns justice.
If a child lives with security, he learns to have faith.
If a child lives with approval, he learns to like himself.
If a child lives with acceptance and friendship, he learns to find love in the world.

Modeling Exercise

Focus in on three modeled behaviors, similar to the two illustrated, that you want to add to your repertoire. In the lefthand column, describe the behavior. In the middle column, list what you presently would expect might happen as a result of using that behavior. Review those expectations carefully; then write your revisions in the righthand column.

New Behavioral Model	Present Expectancy	Revised Expectancy
I want to be able to say no, firmly and immediately, to things I do not want to do.	I will be rejected by others; I will be seen as selfish; I will feel guilty. If I am rejected it will be awful.	I will be able to choose responsibly, to act freely in my own interest, and others may respect my right to say no. If they dislike me, I will be sad but not crushed or guilty.
I want to be free to be open and self-disclosing in genuine and appropriate ways with my friends.	If other people know what I am really like, they will think less of me. If they know personal facts they will use them against me.	The better others come to know me, the more they will like me. If I trust others, they are most likely to be trustworthy, and few will betray a trust.

New Behavioral Model	Present Expectancy	Revised Expectancy

Experiencing Self-Reinforcement

What you expect, you are likely to become. What you predict, you may well do. The expectancies expressed in your habitual thought behavior tend to shape how you act and react. To become aware of your negative expectancies, list them in one column, then rewrite these habitual "bad news" lines into "good news." Learn the new lines, substitute them, tongue in cheek, whenever the old lines occur. The samples below will give you a start.

Negative Expectancies	*Positive Expectancies*
WHEN STRESS IS COMING UP . . .	
"I'm going to be caught off guard and embarrassed."	"I can trust myself to deal with whatever comes up."
"I'm going to worry and worry until the moment arrives."	"I will intentionally rehearse positive responses with confidence."
"I will get more and more anxious until I am frozen with fear."	"I will become more and more eager and excited to begin."
"I will be overwhelmed, uptight, and scared speechless."	"If I feel anxious, I will say so, since describing the feeling helps to dissipate it."
WHEN DIFFICULTIES ARE CROWDING IN . . .	
"I've got to be aware of everything that could happen."	"I need only to focus in on one step at a time."

"I'm feeling tight inside; I have butterflies, and I'm short of breath."

"I will breathe deeply, regularly, and relax intentionally."

"The worst thing possible that can happen, will happen."

"I am free to scare myself with catastrophic fears, or to reassure myself by expecting something better."

"I can't help flashing ahead and worrying about what might be going wrong in the future."

"I can focus on what is happening now, on what I am doing—thinking—feeling now."

WHEN I'M WORKING THROUGH THINGS . . .

"I should have done better."

"I did well enough."

"I must keep warning myself against letting up on my efforts."

"I can afford to be pleased with my work."

"Nothing went wrong this time, but it could have!"

"I worried in vain; I can trust myself to do well enough."

"I carried it off this time; my luck can't hold."

"I can congratulate myself on my progress. I can expect to top it the next time."

WHEN REFLECTING ON YOUR EXPECTANCIES . . .

List negatives:

Create positives:

1.

1.

2.

2.

3.

3.

Chapter 13.
BECOMING IMPACTFUL
Steps to Assertive Change

One year ago . . .

"Do you have anything scheduled for this weekend?" John Myers asks innocently enough. No sooner have I admitted that my schedule is free than he launches into a persuasive request that I give three addresses on marriage on days I have planned to spend enriching my own marriage. I couldn't say no to anyone so sincere and nice, especially after all the appreciation for my work that he has expressed.

An hour later I am *aware* of how easily John has talked me into the appointment. And I'm resenting the loss of my only free weekend of the month . . . and I'm thinking of what I could have said . . . aware, but only in hindsight.

Six months ago . . .

"Do you have the first weekend in September free?" a friend asks. I admit that I do and suddenly realize that I don't. He has excellent plans for my services—excellent as measured by his goals and responsibilities, that is.

I'm *aware* as I agree to his requests that I really want the time for something else . . . I can *identify* what I want to say, I mention my mixed feelings but allow myself to be talked into the commitment anyway. I'm aware at the moment, identifying an alternative, but . . .

Three months ago . . .

"The folks here really appreciated your talks on marriage and family last year. They would like to have a workshop to go deeper into marriage communication. They trust you, and they won't take no for an answer. Which free weekend this month or next will you give us?" I immediately recognize the smooth tones of John Myers and am recalling last year's good experience with his community as well as my frustrating schedule that month.

I'm *aware* of my responses to Reverend Myers, and able to *identify* my old nonassertive niceness that would be falsely agreeable, and I'm now willing to clarify our past relationship and attempt to *negotiate*.

"Perhaps I wasn't clear with you about last year's scheduling. I allowed you to persuade me into giving up my own family time to do those addresses. I'm remembering the frustration I caused myself and my family by agreeing to that. I do not have any truly free weekends in the next six months. I can recommend an associate, or we could plan something next spring."

Awareness, clear identification of my own behaviors and feelings, and a willingness to negotiate past conflicts and affirm openness to the future is a big step into affirmative-assertive living.

Last month . . .

"We need your help immediately. There's so much conflict under the surface in our congregation that I'm afraid it's going to break open—destructively—at any moment. We want you to meet with us for several sessions to get the differences on the table without a blowup." The request is from a pastor I know well and would like to assist, but I know it would require the sacrifice of time I need for my work, that I want for my family, that I'd like for myself.

I have a choice. I can (1) recommend a trusted associate, (2) refer the caller to an associate and work out the arrangements, (3) agree to arrange my schedule in a way partially satisfactory to us both, or (4) firmly and gently refuse the invitation. Having a choice frees me to negotiate and to seek a solution maximally satisfactory to us both. Awareness, identification, negotiation, and immediate pre-

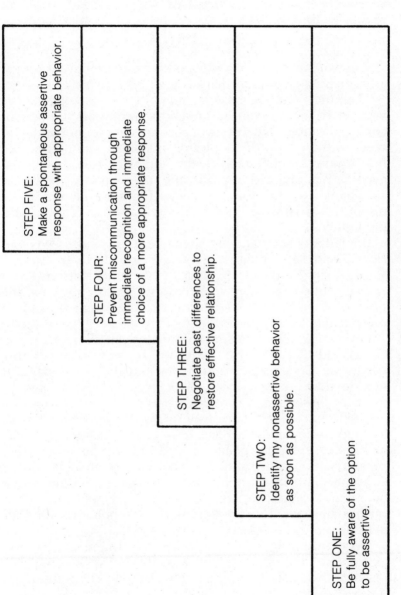

STEP FIVE:
Make a spontaneous assertive response with appropriate behavior.

STEP FOUR:
Prevent miscommunication through immediate recognition and immediate choice of a more appropriate response.

STEP THREE:
Negotiate past differences to restore effective relationship.

STEP TWO:
Identify my nonassertive behavior as soon as possible.

STEP ONE:
Be fully aware of the option to be assertive.

STEPS TO ASSERTIVE CHANGE

vention of misunderstanding free me to be clearly assertive and fully affirmative.

Last week . . .

"Do you have anything planned for this Sunday evening?" an acquaintance asks as he calls me with a request.

"Tell me what you have in mind," I reply spontaneously without either committing myself or cutting off the flow of communication. He offers an interesting opportunity to meet with a group of couples on marriage communication, but I know immediately I do not want to sacrifice the evening planned with my wife and daughters.

"Thank you for the invitation. I'm sure I'd enjoy the opportunity. However, I'm wanting that evening to be with my family."

Immediate, spontaneous openness to my own needs and clear response to another's request provide their own rewards for me and clear honesty for the other person.

These five basic steps to behavioral change describe the process of relearning old behaviors by breaking it down into manageable steps.

Learning a new behavior seldom happens all in one piece. Occasionally an effective model will be seen so clearly that the whole picture snaps into focus and the viewer says, "I can do that; in fact, I can do it even better." In such a moment of closure, a complex of several behaviors may be learned almost simultaneously, in much the same way we learned to ride a bicycle. Seeing in another rider the model of balance, steering, pedaling, and braking integrated, the person may learn from the observation and then turn awareness into action. When a parent places the child on the bike seat, steadies the bike for a hundred yards, and then pushes him off for the solo ride, a whole sequence of behaviors may be grasped in a moment.

More often, behaviors are learned fragmentarily and assembled in a final act of learning. In swimming, for instance, first a face-first-float is mastered. The flutter kick follows; then breathing in and out of water and the long strokes of the arms are added, and the crawl is complete.

The gradual sequence of learning bit on bit, behavior after behavior, is the more common way of achieving assertiveness. And the adding of step on step often proves the more effective way of accumulating new responses and effecting stable, long-lasting change.

The five basic steps of growth which occur in the movement from habitual nonassertive to freely assertive behavior are: awareness, identification, reconciliation, prevention, and spontaneity. Study the charts of these sequential steps carefully, noting the step-by-step addition of building blocks to growth in being immediate and impactful.

The half-steps are where difficulty most often occurs. To be stuck between steps is to be aware of new options, eager to attempt the new behavior, but still slipping back into nonassertive avoidance, escape, or postponing. Awareness makes action possible, but growth is best facilitated by observing effective models and receiving positive reinforcement from the self or from others.

Victor Allen, a physician, had developed a frustrating habit of "thinking shop" and "talking shop" at all times, which slowly drove his wife, Karen, to distraction. Vic decided to cut out all shop talk at home, and be present with his family rather than staying emotionally on the job.

One evening soon after his resolution, Karen and Vic were entertaining another couple, one of whom is also a physician, and Vic got back into an hour of straight medical review.

The next day Vic suddenly realized what he had done and wondered how Karen had felt about it. He checked it out with her only to discover that she had been into such a fascinating conversation with the other partner she hadn't noticed.

In this situation Vic is showing clear movement through steps one to three. He has always been peeved at people who rudely talk about an exclusive subject and shut out others in a group. Now he is coming to awareness of his own inappropriate behavior (first step). His identification of this particular instance came a day late (step one and one-half), but he moved to immediate reconciliation (step three and

STEPS TO ASSERTIVE CHANGE

SPONTANEITY
Spontaneous assertive behavior flows naturally and effectively.

STEP FIVE:
Make a spontaneous assertive response with appropriate behavior.

PREVENTION
Awareness of inappropriate behavior becomes so immediate I can recognize it at thinking level and choose a better alternative.

STEP FOUR:
Prevent miscommunication through immediate recognition and immediate choice of a more appropriate response.

RECONCILIATION
Awareness and identification of my responses free me to attempt a fair solution and to attempt open reconciliation of the tense relationship.

STEP THREE:
Negotiate past differences to restore effective relationship.

IDENTIFICATION
Once aware, I can begin to identify inappropriate behavior when I emit it in my behavioral repertoire and to shorten the delay time in recognizing it.

STEP TWO:
Identify my nonassertive behavior as soon as possible.

AWARENESS
I become aware of assertive responses and of the nature of nonassertive or aggressive copouts (acting too weakly) or blowouts (acting too strongly).

STEP ONE:
Be fully aware of the option to be assertive.

one-half). Fortunately, his fears were groundless since the others had also formed a twosome so reconciliation could have been immediate if necessary at all.

Vic, hopefully, if positively reinforced, will be even more successful in his progression toward assertive behavior change. After this, he will more readily identify his behavior in social situations where the temptation to talk shop occurs spontaneously, and he can take appropriate action in a new response.

It is helpful to examine the five basic steps toward behavior change in more detail. As we work through the sequence from awareness to spontaneous assertiveness, refer to the charts as necessary.

Step I. Awareness

Awareness is the basis of effective change. Some behaviors may be caught by unaware contagion. If you spend much time with someone who is constantly scratching, you will start itching too. But behavior change is rooted in aware choice.

Becoming aware of another's inappropriate behavior is only a half step, but it is the beginning of growth. To be able to label another's response as nonassertive can speed your own growth toward identification of your own inappropriate actions. To report your label to the other is not likely to be well received or growth-producing.

To read, digest, and assimilate this book will provide the first full step of achieving awareness. To be able to apply it in clear identification in most cases will require experiencing the exercises. To advance beyond step two will demand your involvement in applying the new options as you work through misunderstandings, conflicts, and differences to effect reconciliation and new closeness.

The goal of assertively channeling conflicts may require a period of years to reach, but each step forward will release new power to negotiate, relate, and be spontaneously yourself.

Assertive channeling is simply being aware of what you

value and being alert to ways of stating your position firmly and affirmatively. This does not include being abrasive, hostile, rejecting, attacking, or offensive in any way. True assertive channeling can be practiced with courtesy, empathy, and mutuality. To state your true position, you must be able to focus clearly on what your demands are. You must know what you feel, think, and want before you can assert anything.

Becoming aware of over-controlled, nonassertive behavior patterns requires careful growth in self-awareness. Since control is often so automatic, the nonassertive person may have limited awareness of his or her automatic passive response styles. Frequently others reward the nonassertive person by praising his or her patience and controlled endurance. But underneath the gentle exterior may lurk a very frustrated person, not the calm, congenial soul others take for granted.

To become assertive in affirmative channeling, one must (1) become clearly aware of his or her own unassertive behavior, (2) become fully convinced of its unadaptive and useless nature, and (3) bring awareness and insight up to date so immediate action is possible in choosing new responses here and now.

Step II. Identification

Hindsight is $20/20$ in identifying one's own behavior patterns, but the delay can be costly. Six months later I may look back and suddenly realize what went wrong in a conflict that was totally confusing at the time. When I can shorten this delay time to six weeks, to six days, or, better yet, to six hours, I can be more effective. Six minutes is much more useful since I may still be in conversation with the person I have just attacked or appeased. Eventually I may learn to identify my aggressive behavior in six seconds, and be able to change my response in midsentence. The longer the delay time in reflecting on what I am doing and how I am doing it, the less free I am to change and grow. Growth happens here. Now. As I am aware of what I am doing here and now.

Step III. Reconciliation

So long as I am still identifying my nonassertive behavior after the fact, I must attempt a delayed reconciliation. Belatedly I may contact the party with whom I was assertive and attempt to reconcile the disrupted relationship. (Nonassertive or aggressive behaviors invariably disrupt relationships.) Reconciliation after the fact is doubly difficult in that healing must be found for the original pain and for the accumulated resentment and hurt. Going back and discussing the problem with the hurt person is extremely difficult, since each person's memory has either enlarged or explained away the facts. Time heals some hurts, but it makes others hurt even more. Immediate reconciliation—as immediate as possible—is wisdom.

As soon as the unsuitable behavior is seen for what it is, immediate attempts should be made to clarify the relationship, restore the trust, and return to spontaneous openness with each other once more. Recognition can be followed by immediate reconciliation. If I am aware enough to recognize on the spot that I have said something aggressive, I can immediately admit that I am coming across aggressively. If, on the other hand, I do not identify my aggression until some time later, I can still go to the person and reconcile as soon as I am aware of the need to do so.

Step IV. Immediate Prevention

Once I have learned to be aware of what I'm doing as I'm doing it, I can begin to recognize nonassertive or aggressive behaviors on a new level. Now I can think about my behavior rather than identifying it only after having acted it out. This inserts some distance between the stimulus and the response (S→R). Too little distance between the stimulus—the other person's behavior—and my response results in my using habitual or reflexive behavior. Reflexes learned in early childhood can be painfully childish unless adulthood has reconditioned them. The old admonition, "Count to ten before you speak," is not enough. We must think clearly about what will be said and done in order to be assertive rather than nonassertive or aggressive. Holding your own mental behavioral rehearsals is excellent preparation for times when emotion is high. Habitual rehearsing, however, is equally as bad as never rehearsing. A person who constantly rehearses all communications sounds like a recorded announcement. When an internal editor censors all messages, the warmth of immediacy is lost.

Step V. Spontaneity

Spontaneous selection of assertive behaviors is a natural result of affirm-and-assert training, but it is not a necessary goal. The ability deliberately to select an appropriate response by thinking on your feet may be better than being spontaneously assertive in every situation. In low-risk situations, however, where it is safe for us to be naturally assertive, we may be more spontaneous. But even a positive and effective conditioned response needs to be examined in confusing situations so the most responsible choice can be made. When situations change rapidly and each situation is different, an automatic, stereotyped response may rather quickly be unadaptive.

Since most natural reinforcers in our society act as negative reinforcers, behavior must usually occur in the face of or against negative reinforcement. Since most of us have had so much negative conditioning, we almost invariably respond negatively to negative stimuli. Being assertive requires our being vigilant and continually volitional to overcome the numerous negative stimuli we face. We must free ourselves to choose the most appropriate available response now, to select what fits here, in this situation.

Hillel, the great rabbi who lived and taught from 70 B.C. to A.D. 10, summed up assertive and affirmative living in an Aramaic poem (which rhymes perfectly in the original).

> If I am not for myself
>> Who will be for me?
> If I am for myself alone,

What am I?
If not now, when?

"If I am not for myself, who will be for me?" is a manifesto for assertiveness. I am unquestionably for me. If I think, act, speak in negatives, who will interrupt my self-depreciation and slow self-destruction?

"If I am not for myself alone, what am I?" is a mandate for affirmation. To be human is to ground my acts in equal respect and regard, and to guard relationships with another in equal rights and responsibilities.

"If not now, when?" is a motivation to act now. It is to begin from where I am in this moment, step by step, to grow toward maturity as a person in each interpersonal relationship.

Experiencing Steps to Assertive and Affirmative Change

Examine the following case situation and, using the same numbers used in the subheads in this chapter, identify the steps toward more immediate awareness and responsible action:

SITUATION ONE:

_____ Jim B. is a salesman who has a knack at moving cars no one else can get off the lot. At home he is equally smooth, persuasive, and invariably nice. When his wife, Jeri, is tense or unhappy with his work schedule, Jim agrees with her criticisms, promises to change, but continues to let everyone impose on him. "It's good for business," he explains. It is not good for Jim's stomach.

_____ One evening Jeri is angry that he is an hour late, as is often the case. When he arrives home, she ventilates her irritation with a whole series of trapping questions. Jim smiles, swallows his own frustration, and withdraws into silence, unaware that his constant stomach pains are doubling as he smiles his way through her criticisms.

_____ Acute ulcers are the signal that alerts Jim to his internal conflicts, and he begins to recognize his need to assert his own point of view. Unfortunately, his warm smiles are such an automatic response to any conflict situation that it is hours later before he is able to think of other responses he might have made.

_____ Tonight, as Jeri and he are in the midst of a hassle, Jim suddenly realizes what he is doing.

———— "This isn't what I want out of our relationship, Jeri," he says. "I'd like us to respect each other as equals. I feel so distant from you when I'm trying to smile my way out of things. I want to work through things until we're close again. I really do care."

SITUATION TWO—STEPS TOWARD ASSERTING AND AFFIRMING:

Note the sequence of events from paragraphs one through ten; review the steps to assertive change discussed in this chapter to identify fully what is taking place.

Stimulus	Response	Consequence
1. I was in my room when my sister called up the stairs that there was a phone call for me.	2. I didn't make a move, and gave no signal that I had heard her. (Nonassertive response of avoidance)	3. She assumed that I had not heard her call.
4. She climbed the stairs and knocked on my door, calling more loudly.	5. I yelled back, "I heard you the first time; you don't have to yell at me." (Aggressive response of verbal hostility and criticism)	6. She said, "If you heard me, why didn't you tell me the first time?" Her voice is angry in response. (Aggressive reaction)
7. I felt badly because my sister was angry at me when I had acted aggressively in an inappropriate way. (Step Two)	8. I immediately recognized that I had been aggressive and nonaffirmative, but hesitated to admit it to her and seek reconciliation (Step Three)	9. An hour later I expressed my regrets for being insensitive and affirmed that I wanted to be more responsible with her in the future. (Step Three and a Half)

10. I am glad to be back into relationships of respect, and I am determined to respond immediately to clarify misunderstandings. (Anticipation of Step Four)	11. The next conflict situation arises. . . .	12. The result is:

Now reflect on a recent conflict of your own; chart the sequence of events on the next page. Identify the steps to assertive change which occurred in your behavior. Rehearse new responses you can make in future conflicts calling for more effective behaviors.

S ────────────► R ────────────► C

Stimulus ────────► *Response* ──────► *Consequence*

1.

2.

3.

4.

5.

6.

7.

8.

9.

Chapter 14.
CREATING COMMUNITY:
The Goal of Assertive-and-Affirmative Lifestyles

"It's every man for himself in this life. If you don't look out for yourself, nobody else will."

(The speaker believes that every person is ultimately alone in this world. Each must finally trust only himself.)

"In the end, what truly matters is the community that stands with you, the friends that surround you, the circle of people that have helped shape you."

(The speaker believes that every person is truly a part of the community that has shaped, formed, supported his or her growth to personhood.)

Neither is true alone. Both are valid. Each of us is alone in the moment of decision-making. Every person must answer responsibly for his or her choices. But each of us is an expression of the community which nurtured us—a part of the human fabric which helped form our values, views, and belief system. I am my community. I am not my community. Both are true. Or better said, I am a whole community of persons. People known, loved, and prized in my lifetime have entered into my existence, enriching or impoverishing me. Yet I am not just the sum of such experience with others. I am I. I am unique. I am a part of my significant communities. I am a discrete and separate part of that community.

You Are Not Human Alone

To be human is to be in relationships with fellow humans. We are relational beings, we humans, who cannot be truly human alone. A need for community is an essential part of persons. Personhood is a subdivision of peoplehood. I am inescapably a part of that small section of the human family which created the unique blend of experiences that are me.

If I assert myself at my community's expense, I am poorer, not richer, as a result. To exploit the relationships which create me is to harm myself.

If I negate myself for my community's benefit as a continuing sacrifice of selfhood, I am depriving them of my full strength. I am defrauding myself of the privilege of being all I can be with those who people my life.

The significant people of my life deserve to have my full strength exercised in our community interrelationships. By being assertive, I am offering them a solid, candid, genuine person to rely on, to conflict with, to care about. By being affirmative I am providing them with a warm, appreciative person to trust, to value.

You Are Not Mature Alone

Of all the models of human maturity, only those who are communitarian take the whole person seriously. It is not enough to be a man of impactful and successful behavior, or a woman with a fully functioning personality, unless the impact increases the quality of loving relationships, or the functioning deepens the richness of life in community.

Maturity, by the definition we have been using in this study, is to be mastering relational skills so naturally that we can effectively achieve a positively reinforcing lifestyle that expresses what is in our best interest and equally at the interest of the community around us.

Maturity is achieving the freedom to experience all our rights as persons while fully respecting the equal rights of our fellows. It is asserting our own power and affirming the equal potential for others.

Four Freedoms—Four Rights

Asserting and affirming, when expressed simultaneously, safeguard the four freedoms of human relationships that are essential to intrapersonal and interpersonal wholeness.

1. You are free to assert equal rights with others; you are right to affirm equal freedom for others.

2. You are right to regard yourself as equally worthful with others; you are free to regard others as equally valuable with you.

3. You are right to respect your own integrity as a person; you are free to respect the equal integrity of others.

4. You are right to own responsibility for your thoughts, words, actions; you are free to respect others' equal responsibility for their thoughts, words, and acts.

Freedom One: Equal Rights

I have the right to say yes and no. I have the privilege of thinking, feeling, choosing, and acting for myself, and to enjoy or suffer the consequences of my thoughts, emotions, choices, and actions.

Each of us is created to be the initiator, evaluator, and administrator of his or her own behavior as a rightful community member and a responsible community-maker.

I have the right to initiate my own behavior—to choose what I value, prize, and want. (If my desires, wants, and greed seek to usurp another's rights, I have overextended my freedom and invaded another's lifespace, and I am violating community.)

I have the right to evaluate my own behavior, to determine what is desirable and undesirable, to judge what is good and what is bad. (If my judgment runs into conflict with the accepted law of my community, then I have challenged the common trust of my fellows and must accept the consequences. If I should become so dominated or absorbed by my community that I have no freedom to say yes or no, I impoverish self and others.)

I have the right to administrate my own choices. I can determine my use of time by saying yes and no to invitations, expectations, or demands. I can define my use of distance by deciding who is close to me and whom I prefer to keep formal and distant. I can decide what I am willing to do for others and how I will work with authorities, where I will go or act for self or others.

How these rights are worked out with others will vary from situation to situation, from community to community, depending on whether the relationship is vertical, horizontal, or multidirectional.

Relating to public community authorities tends to occur essentially as a vertical relationship in which communication is a reaching up to a higher functional level or down to a lower. That is, when I appeal to the city for rights to build a house, I represent one family and I appeal to the next level up, which includes a village of families. Thus communication is vertical in "you can" and "you cannot" terms. Equal rights are guaranteed.

Relating in private communities as fellow adults such as with marriage partners, associates, siblings, or parents tends to be horizontal. Here equal rights must be negotiated and no set definitions can be formulated for the rapidly changing situations.

Relating in formal business relationships tends to be multidirectional and defined by the nature of the contract and the exchange of valuables. Such commercial relationships operate in multidirectional ways as negotiated by the parties involved, and rights are defined by the nature of the agreements that are made.

Assertiveness presses for human rights to the fullest possible capacity for all persons. Thus in vertical relationships, full available rights will be claimed. In horizontal relationships, equal rights will be affirmed. In formal public and business relationships, optimal rights in social and commercial justice will be sought.

Human presumptuousness and authoritarian usurping of power over others will be confronted. The "divine right of kings" to impose their will on less privileged peasants went unquestioned for long periods in Western civilization. But the conviction could not be stifled that all persons are "endowed by their Creator with certain inalienable rights" which are equally respected by the common law of human communities. Claiming these rights is the privilege of each person who values justice and seeks to model it for the good of self and others.

Freedom One: Equal Rights

I am free to choose my words and acts;
Therefore free to change and grow.

I am free to be spontaneous;
Therefore free to make mistakes.

I am free to trust my hunches;
Therefore free to be illogical.

I am free to be flexible;
Therefore free to change my mind.

I am free to live by my own supports;
Therefore free to refuse help and kindness.

I am free to take the consequences for my acts;
Therefore free to offer no justification for my choices.

I am free to love and care for others;
Therefore free to tell you without permission.

I am free to want relationships;
Therefore free to reach out for contact.

Freedom Two: Equal Regard

"Love," poet Robert Frost once whimsically observed, "is an irresistible desire to be irresistibly desired." As a drive toward relatedness, love is a powerful attraction toward another who is seen as worthful and desirable.

When love is dependent upon a person's external appearance, ability, or performance, it tends to be conditional upon the continuance of that attractiveness, talent, or achievement. Internal love transcends such conditional approval to prize the other as the unique and changing person he or she truly is. Such love honors, values, respects, and encourages the other's thrust as an unfolding precious and worthful creation apart from imposed conditions or demanded prescriptions for behavior.

This is the heart of all truly human love which is grounded in the value of humankind. It is loving another as I love myself. To do this, I must see the other as equal in value—as irreducibly valuable, precious, and worthful even as I know myself to be. The most accurate words to define such love are "equal regard."

The nature of such mature love has been defined in many partially true ways. It is frequently described as benevolence: "To love even the unlovely and the unlovable," but such a stance belittles the beloved. The other may be unloved or unloving but not unlovable. It is often defined as self-sacrifice: "To love the other at one's own expense since the other must always come first." Self-sacrifice can be incredibly self-righteous and motivated solely by the lover's need to play superior and controlling in a very humble but strategic way.

Equal regard may be benevolent, but not in denigration of the other. It gives, asking for no return in a situation where generosity is an appropriate expression of the equal worth of both or all concerned. Equal regard may choose to act in a self-forgetful and sacrificial way, but only when this is a true forgoing of self-fulfillment for the sake of human fulfillment or for the good of both or all the parties concerned. The value is not placed in the act of sacrifice, but rather in the prizing of both self and other equally.

Self-sacrifice, benevolence, altruism all tend to become absorbing rather than affirming. The balance of affirmation is best protected in the equal regard which sees the other as equally worthful with the self, neither inferior nor superior in spite of all differences, but equally worthful.

This is loving the neighbor as the self, prizing the other person as we prize our own persons, affirming the equal worth of both self and other as infinite in value, of ultimate worth. We can stand with each other with equal respect and equal responsibility and celebrate our equal rights as persons of dignity, integrity, and irreducible value. That is, nothing can increase or decrease the value of persons. A person's behavior may be viewed as appropriate or inappropriate, as functional or dysfunctional, as of no social value or socially valuable. But this in no way alters the value of the person emitting that behavior. Each of us is precious and worthful simply because we are we.

Freedom Two: Equal Regard

I am irreducibly valuable.
  You are irreducibly valuable.

I am worthy of being loved
  simply because I am I.

You are worthy of being loved
  only because you are you.

I am precious and worthful
  as I am, not as I act.

You are worthful, valuable
  as you are, not as you earn it.

My freedom to be me
  is infinitely precious to me.

Your freedom to be you
  is equally precious to me.

I will not see me as superior to you.
I will not see you as inferior to me.
  Or vice versa. Or verse vica.

You are you and I am I.
As we see each other
  with agape—equal regard—we are we.

This is to love the other as the self
  and to prize the self with every other.

Freedom Three: Equal Responsibility

I do not cause another's unhappiness. No one else is the cause of mine. I make me miserable with my demands that things be different than they are, that I be different than I am. To believe that I am responsible for the unhappiness of others and they are responsible for mine leads to emotional absorption.

Each of us is able to respond as a self only for that self.

The fantasy that I can be response-able for another is vainly presumptuous. If I fantasize that I can control other's emotions and "make" them angry, happy, or sad, I'm likely to begin thinking I have power over their other choices and behavior as well. And with power comes responsibility. But I do not have the ability to respond for you. Your responses are yours. My responses are mine.

If I become unhappy with you, I do it for my own reasons. Perhaps I do not approve of your behavior, so I can make myself unhappy with my demands that you change. Maybe I do not like your responses to me, so I may make myself miserable with demands that you live as I prescribe. My unhappiness comes from my refusal to love, to prize you as you are, to be willingly happy with you as you. My unhappiness comes from my judgments about what you do and who you are. My labels become a liability to my appreciation of you. To love you is to enjoy you for being you. And to enjoy your enjoyment of being enjoyed.

To affirm my equal response-ability with you is to recognize that I am free to respond to you in loving or unloving ways, and for that I am responsible. You are equally free to do so to me, and for that you are fully responsible. This is an affirmation of my ability to be me and of your equal ability to be you. It is a compliment to my integrity and an equally good word for yours.

To assert my equal responsibility is to refuse to be talked into being dependent on you and needing you to be dependent on me. (A parasitic relationship goes both ways. There is both parasitic dependence and parasitic dominance. To be underresponsible is to stick you with the credit for my behavior; to be overresponsible is to be willingly stuck with yours.) I can say no freely. I can say yes genuinely. I can respond to you with all my ability while simultaneously respecting and encouraging your equal ability—equal response-ability.

FREEDOM THREE: EQUAL RESPONSIBILITY

I own
My experience of me.

You may own
Your experience of you.

The thoughts I think,
The feelings I feel,
The perceptions I see,
The judgments I make,
The values I hold,

The thoughts you think,
The feelings you feel,
The perceptions you see,
The judgments you make,
The values you hold,

Are mine and for them
I am always responsible.

Are yours and for them
I am in no way responsible.

I own
My expression of me.

You may own
Your expression of you.

The words I speak,
The signals I show,
The love I confess,
The anger I emit,
The actions I take,
The behaviors I use,

The words you speak,
The signals you show,
The love you express,
The anger you emit,
The actions you take,
The behaviors you use,

Are mine and for them
I am always responsible.

Are yours and for them
I am in no way responsible.

Freedom Four: Equal Respect

I will not disrespect your integrity as a person by attempting to credit or fault you with honor or guilt for my behaviors.

I will respect you by truly respecting me. As I am all that I can be when I am with you, I invite you to be all you can possibly be in relationship with me.

Such respect sees the equal power and potential in the other, whether exercised with success or failure. When relationships are successful, each has equal cause for celebration. When there is failure, the conflict will be defined mutually; any responsibility will be laid between us as a problem to be negotiated, not as blame to be decided.

We will end blaming games. I am always responsible for my behavior; I am never to blame. You are always responsible for your behavior; you are never to blame. "Blame" is an interpersonal transaction in which the responsibility for one person's behavior is laid at another's doorstep. Responsibility is a mutually defined process which recognizes shared ownership of any two-person relationship.

Any effective resolution of conflict depends upon the ability of parties involved to define the problem mutually. It takes two people to have a problem. Problems are invariably interpersonal dysfunctions. To define a situation mutually provides a basis for effective negotiation in which the needs, wants, and hopes of each are equally respected.

FREEDOM FOUR: EQUAL RESPECT

I will respond to you
as I respond for myself:

> I will neither blame you for my actions nor accept blame for yours.

> I will neither justify and excuse my choices nor expect a defense for yours.

```
THE LOVELESS              A                    THE NO-RIGHTS
COMMUNITY                 B                 COMMUNITY WHERE
WHERE THE                 S                    THE PRIVILEGES
EQUAL WORTH               O                    OF PERSONHOOD
OF SELF AND               R            ARE NEITHER ASSERTED
OTHER IS NOT              B                   FOR THE SELF OR
VALUED AND PRIZED         I              AFFIRMED FOR OTHERS
                          N
                          G

                     CREATIVE

                          A
                          F
                          F
                          I
NONASSERTIVE     ASSERTING              AGGRESSIVE
                          M
                          I
                          N
                          G

                     COMMUNITY

                          N
                          O
                          N
                          A
                          F
                          F
                          I                  THE IRRESPONSIBLE
THE DISRESPECTFUL         R                 COMMUNITY WHERE
COMMUNITY WHERE           M            MATURE BEHAVIOR OF
THE INTEGRITY OF          I             SELF AND OTHER ARE
SELF OR OTHER IS          N               NEITHER MODELED
VIOLATED OR IGNORED       G                  NOR REINFORCED
```

I will neither demand you live up to my expectations nor commit myself to live up to yours.

I will respect you
as I respect myself:

I will openly admit my failures and be candid and respectful with yours.

I will be flexibly willing to negotiate and adjust my behavior and seek solutions satisfying to us both.

I will assert my concern for equal rights and affirm my commitment to equal respect.

Creative community brings together wholeness for people, invites wholeness to emerge from people, excites its people to experience all they can be with each other.

Creative community does not occur unless people prize community enough to risk asserting their wholeness with others by living as though such a human fabric of equal regard, equal respect, equal rights, and equal responsibility exists here now. As you and I live in such a fulfilled mature way, the community has begun. Where two persons contract to honor each other with such reality, community is real. Where a growing circle of persons work at such integrity of loving and living, community is being born and being nurtured into the wholeness which we humans are created and gifted to experience.

Maturity is measured by a person's prizing of human community. To assert human rights with others, to affirm human worth with others is to be truly human as a person of dignity and worth.

Be that person.

Act new. Act now.

Relaxation Exercise

Dominant behavior inhibits less dominant behavior. If the dominant response is tenseness and anxiety, this will flood and dominate all awareness. If the dominant response is relaxation, this will be the internal state. If relaxation is preferred to tension, then it can be learned so well that it becomes the dominant response. By practicing one of the following muscle relaxation exercises two or three times a day, the reader can learn to will such complete relaxation that the tension-reduction sequence becomes unnecessary. These techniques, originated by Dr. Edmond Jacobsen in 1938, Joseph Wolpe in 1958 (with later publications in 1964, 1969, and 1973) and numerous therapists since, have proven effective in intervening in chronic anxiety, headaches, phobias, high blood pressure, and hypertensive states.

Included here is a set of muscle relaxation exercises.

There are least three ways of using the instructions. First, you can read through the instructions to try to relax. This is the least effective way to relax because one is actually stimulated to some degree by having to concentrate on reading. The second way is to have someone else read the instructions to you while you try to relax. This can be effective, but it gets rather tedious and monotonous for the reader to go through the instructions repetitiously. The third way is to record the instructions on a cassette or other tape and then just practice by replaying the tape and following the instructions.*

When reading the instructions either for practicing muscle relaxation or for recording, read slowly, softly, and gently. The series of periods indicate pauses. The more periods, the longer the pauses. This is to allow time for the body to experience relaxation while doing the exercise.

---

*Professionally recorded cassette tapes may be ordered for $9.95 each from AUGMENT, 3035 S. Gaylord, Denver, CO 80210.

Progressive Muscle Relaxation Instructions

The instructions that follow will teach you how to relax yourself whenever you feel tense. Even though you may not feel anything, I want you to follow the instructions step by step. As you do so you will learn how to relax.

Make yourself comfortable either in a reclining chair or lying down. As you do that I want you to settle back as comfortably as you can, close your eyes, and get yourself relaxed to the best of your ability. . . . As you relax like that, clench your right fist, just clench your fist tighter and tighter, and feel the tension as you do so, now relax. . . . Let the fingers of your right hand become loose and observe the contrast in your feelings. . . . Just let yourself go and try to become more relaxed all over. . . . Once more, clench your right fist rather tight; squeeze it down, hold it and notice the tension; feel the tension in your right fist, your hand, your forearm. . . . All right, now let go. Just relax. Let your fingers straighten out. . . . Notice the difference once more. . . . Now repeat that with your left fist. Clench your left fist while the rest of your body relaxes. . . . Clench the fist tighter and feel the tension. . . . Now relax. . . . Again, enjoy the contrast. . . . . Repeat that once more. . . . Make that left fist tight and tense. . . . . . Hold it tight. . . . Now do the opposite of tension. . . . Relax. . . . Feel the difference. . . . Just continue relaxing like that for a while. . . . . . Now clench both fists; clench them tighter, and feel the tension in your forearms. Study the sensations; feel the cramping, the aching. . . . Relax. . . . . Straighten out your fingers and feel the relaxation. . . . Continue to relax. . . . Just relax your hands and forearms more and more. . . . . .

Now bend your elbows and tense your biceps. . . . Tense them harder. . . . Study the tension. . . . All right, straighten out your arms; let them relax and feel the difference again. . . . Just let the relaxation develop. . . . . Say to yourself, "I feel warm and relaxed, warm and relaxed." . . . . . Once more tense your biceps again. . . . Hold the tension; hold it tight, and observe it carefully. . . . . Now straighten out your arms; relax. . . . Relax to the best of your ability. . . . . . . Just relax your arms back to a comfortable position and let the relaxation proceed to the rest of your body. . . . . Your arms should feel comfortably heavy if you allow them to relax. . . . Concentrate on the true relaxation of the arms without any tension. . . . Get them comfortable; just let them relax further and further. . . . Even when your arms seem fully relaxed, try to go that extra little bit further. . . . Try to achieve deeper and deeper levels of relaxation. . . . . Concentrate on letting all your muscles go loose and heavy. . . . . Say out loud, "My muscles feel warm, loose and heavy." . . . "My muscles feel warm, loose, and heavy." . . .

Wrinkle up your forehead now; wrinkle it tighter, still tighter. Feel the tension in your forehead. Just hold it. . . . . Now stop; stop wrinkling your forehead. Relax and smooth it out. . . . Let the entire forehead become smooth as the forehead continues to relax. . . . Just let it flatten out. . . . . . Now frown, crease your brows, study this tension as you frown hard. . . . . . . Now let go of the tension. . . . . Smooth out your forehead once more. . . . Just let it flatten out and relax. . . . Feel the relief of tension as you relax. . . . Relax, relax. . . .

Now close your eyes tight. . . . Pull them tighter and feel the tension. . . . . Just feel the tension. . . . Now relax, relax, completely. Just let completely go. . . . Keep your eyes gently and comfortably closed. . . . . Notice the relaxation around your eyes. . . . . Now clench your jaw. . . Bite your teeth together. . . Bite hard. Study the tension throughout the jaw. . . . Study the tension in your cheek muscles. . . . . . Now relax your jaw. . . . Appreciate the relaxation. . . . . . Feel the relaxation all over your face, all over your forehead, your eyes, your jaw, your lips, your tongue. . . . Let the relaxation progress further and further, deeper and deeper. . . . Repeat out loud, "My face feels heavy, warm, and relaxed." . . . "My face feels heavy, warm, and relaxed." . . .

Now tense your front neck muscles. Make a "web" neck. . . . Now relax. . . . Relax. . . . Relax. . . . Press your head back as hard as you can and feel the tension in the back of the neck. . . . Now let your head return forward to a comfortable position. . . . Study the relaxation. . . . Just let the relaxation develop. . . . . . . Feel that nice, warm, heavy feeling. . . . Shrug your shoulders up now. Shrug them up hard; just bring them right up and hold the tension. . . . . Drop your shoulders now and feel the relaxation; feel the relaxation in your neck, your shoulders. . . . Just let them completely drop down. . . . . Shrug your shoulders again; feel the tension in your shoulders and your back. . . . . Drop your shoulders once more. . . . Let the relaxation spread deep within your shoulders, right into your back muscles. . . . Relax your neck, throat, your jaw, and all the other facial muscles as pure relaxation takes over. Just let it go deeper and deeper and deeper. . . . . Just relax your entire body to the best of your ability. . . . . Feel the comfortable heaviness that accompanies relaxation. . . . . . Just breathe easily and freely i-n and o-u-t. Regularly, deeply, slowly, and rhythmically i-n and o-u-t. . . . . Notice how the relaxation increases as you exhale. . . . As you breathe out just feel the relaxation. . . . . .

Now breathe in and fill your lungs again; inhale deeply and hold your breath; study the tension. . . . . . . All right, now exhale; let the walls of your chest go loose and limp, and let it push the air out automatically. . . . . . Just continue relaxing and breathing gently and rhythmically. Feel the relaxation and enjoy it. . . . Just feel the relaxation every time you let that air blow out. . . . Every time you let your chest fall down, let it push the air out and feel the relaxation. . . . . . . Let the rest of your body relax as much as possible, as you breathe slowly and rhythmically.

Now once again, take a slow, deep breath in-and-hold it. . . . Okay, let your chest collapse. . . . Breathe out and appreciate the release that comes from letting your chest go and push the air out of your lungs. . . . Just breathe normally now. . . regularly and rhythmically. . . .

Continue relaxing your chin. . . . Let the relaxation spread to your back and shoulders, to your neck and arms. Just completely let go. Just let yourself go completely limp. . . . . Next give attention to your abdominal muscles, your stomach area. . . . Tighten your stomach muscles. Push out your stomach muscles, make them hard. . . hard as a board. . . . Notice the tension in your stomach muscles. . . . . Now relax and let the muscles loosen, and notice the contrast. . . . . Once more press and tighten your stomach muscles hard. That's it, hard. Hold it and study the tension in the muscles. . . . Study the tension in the stomach muscles. . . . . . And relax. . . . . . . Notice the general well-being that comes with relaxing your stomach. . . . . Now tense your stomach. . . . Feel the tension. . . . . And relax again. . . . . . Continue breathing normally and equally. . . . . Now this time pull your stomach in and hold it in tension. . . . Hold it hard. . . . Hold and feel the tension. . . . . Okay, now relax. . . . Just let your stomach muscles relax. . . . Let the tension dissolve into relaxation. . . deeper and deeper. . . . Each time you breathe out notice the rhythmic relaxation both in your chest and stomach. . . . Just let go of all the tension. . . . . Just let yourself go completely limp. . . . And relax. . . . Just feel that sense of well-being. . . that nonchalant "I don't care" attitude. . . . Just let completely go. . . . Feel that relaxation go all over your whole body muscles. . . . . . .

Flex your thighs now. . . . Flex them by pressing on your heels as hard as you can. . . . Feel the tension. . . . Feel the tightness in the back of your thighs. . . . . Press hard. . . . Relax now and note the difference. . . . . Just feel the warmth, the aching sensation in the thighs as you relax completely. . . . Flex your thigh muscles again, and hold the tension; hold it hard. . . . That's it. . . . That's it, hard. . . . Feel the aching in the thigh muscles. . . . . . Now relax; relax your hips and thighs. . . . . Just allow the relaxation to proceed on its own. . . . . Feel the difference. . . that good warm sensation from relaxation in your thighs. . . .

Now press your feet and toes downward away from your face until the calf muscles become tense and tight. . . . Push hard, that's it. . . . Study that tension now. . . . . . Relax, relax now. . . . . . Just feel that warm feeling in the muscles, that tingling sensation. . . . Once again press your feet and toes downward away from your face. . . . . . Let your calf muscles become tense. . . hard, cramping. . . . . Now relax, relax your feet and calves. . . . Keep relaxing like that for awhile. . . . Just let yourself relax further and further all over. . . . Relax your feet, ankles, calves, knees, thighs, hips. . . . Feel the difference in your lower body as you relax still further and further. . . . Feel the warmth and heaviness. . . . Let the relaxation spread to your stomach, your waist, your back. . . . Let go more and more. . . . Just let it go that little bit further, completely relax. . . . Just feel that relaxation all over your body. . . . . Let it proceed to your upper back, chest, shoulders and arms, out to the tips of your fingers. . . . Keep relaxing more and more deeply. . . . Relax your neck, your jaw, and all your facial muscles. . . . Just let them completely relax. . . . Let yourself relax completely. . . . Keep relaxing your whole body like that for awhile. . . . You can become twice as relaxed as you are right now merely by taking a really deep breath. . . . Breathe in deeply. Now hold it. . . . Slowly exhale. . . . Just let your chest walls fall down and push the air out. . . . . Now breathe in deeply once more. Now exhale; feel yourself becoming heavier and heavier. . . . Feel how heavy and relaxed you have become. Breathe slowly, regularly, and rhythmically. . . . Just stay in perfect relaxation. You should not feel any tension from a single muscle in your body. Your whole body becomes progressively heavier and heavier and all your muscles relax. . . . Let go more and more completely. . . . Now give your muscles individual attention. . . . Relax the muscles of your forehead. Just let your entire scalp become smooth. . . . Now relax the muscles in the lower part of your face. . . . . Relax the muscles of your jaw, the muscles of your tongue. . . . Give it attention again. . . . Relax the muscles of your forehead, and of the lower part of your face. . . . Relax the muscles of your jaw. As you do so, your jaw will hang slightly open. . . . Now relax the muscles of your tongue. . . . Relax the muscles of your neck and all of the muscles of your shoulders. . . . Completely relax. . . . Relax the muscles of your trunk and those of your lower limbs. . . . Just let go of any tension you have left; let the relaxation take over completely. . . . Just let yourself relax. . . . .

You feel so much at ease now and so very comfortable. . . . In this state of perfect relaxation you feel completely unwilling to move a single muscle. You feel so lazy, unconcerned, and nonchalant. . . . As you are lying there like that and feel so good, picture the word "relax" and say the word "relax" quietly and rhythmically. Relax. . . . Relax. . . . . . Feel yourself completely limp. . . . Again, picture the word "relax" and once again say "relax." . . . Now say, "I'm calm and relaxed." . . . "I'm calm and relaxed." . . . "My body feels warm and heavy." . . . Do that once more. . . . "I'm calm and relaxed; my body feels warm and heavy. I feel so peaceful and restful. R-e-l-a-x.". . . See the word "relax" and say "relax"; say, "I'm calm and relaxed.". . . . "Relax." . . . Feel yourself completely tranquil, contented, drowsy and lazy, limp and relaxed. . . . Just let yourself feel that totally relaxed, calm, and serene feeling. . . . Relax; say "relax." . . . Relax. . . . Say, "I'm warm, relaxed, drowsy, heavy, tranquil, and lazy. I feel so good, so warm, and so relaxed. . . . . I feel so good, so warm, and so relaxed." . . .

As you are completely relaxed, totally serene, and tranquil, I will count backwards from four to one. When I get to one you will open your eyes to a very refreshed, wide awake, calm, tranquil, and serene feeling. . . . . Four. . . . . . . Three. . . . . . Two. . . . . . . One. . . . . . .

Suggestions for Further Reading

Alberti, R., and Emmons, M. *Your Perfect Right*. San Luis Obispo, CA: Impact Press, 1974.

———. *Stand Up, Speak Out, Talk Back!* New York: Pocket Books, 1975. Two outstanding books on assertively claiming your own rights in interpersonal conflict situations. They provide clear outlines for understanding the crucial differences between assertiveness and aggression.

Augsburger, D. *Anger, Assertiveness, and Pastoral Care*. Philadelphia: Fortress Press, 1979. An exploration of the functions of anger and assertiveness for persons in the helping professions, with special application to the ministry.

———. *Caring Enough to Confront*. Glendale, CA: Regal Books, 1980. A popularly written guide to effective caring and confronting relationships in marriage, family, work, and community situations. Blends psychology and theology for a creative Christian expression of wholeness in personhood.

Bower, G., and Bower, S. *Asserting Yourself: A Practical Guide for Positive Change*. Reading, MA: Addison-Wesley, 1976. An explicit training workbook on behavioral rehearsal and assertive thinking, negotiating, and contracting.

Fensterheim, H., and Baer, J. *Don't Say Yes When You Want to Say No*. New York: David McKay, 1975. A helpful and easy-reading book on assertiveness in widely varied situations with many scripts and scenarios for practicing new behaviors.

Lazarus, A., and Fay, A. *I Can If I Want To*. New York: William Morrow, 1975. An excellent book that describes how a number of irrational myths can keep people from acting assertively. Brief, concise, effective in outlining ways to go about changing self-defeating thoughts and behavior.

Mayeroff, M. *On Caring.* New York: Harper, 1973. The best available book on caring and on the nature of loving relationships which free people to both give and receive support and affection in rewarding relationships.

Phelps, S. and Austin, N. *The Assertive Woman.* San Luis Obispo, CA: Impact Press, 1975. A highly useful training book for assertiveness as a woman in a society that has reinforced nonassertive behavior for females.

Smith, M. *When I Say No, I Feel Guilty.* New York: Bantam Books, 1975. A creative, funny, and at times outrageous method for outmanipulating manipulators by use of assertiveness. High on asserting. Low on affirming.